| | | ∝ | | |

THE ETIQUETTE
OF FREEDOM

**Gary Snyder, Jim Harrison,
and *The Practice of the Wild***

Edited by Paul Ebenkamp

COUNTERPOINT

BERKELEY

Published by arrangement with San Simeon Films.

All photos are used courtesy of San Simeon Films,
except where noted otherwise.

Library of Congress Cataloging-in-Publication Data

Snyder, Gary, 1930–
The etiquette of freedom : Gary Snyder, Jim Harrison,
and The practice of the wild / by Gary Snyder and Jim Harrison.
ISBN-13: 978-1-58243-629-6
ISBN-10: 1-58243-629-0
1. Snyder, Gary. 1930—Interviews. 2. Harrison, Jim, 1937—Interviews.
3. Poets, American—20th century—Interviews. 4. Authors, American—
20th century—Interviews. 5. Beat generation—Interviews.
I. Practice of the wild (Motion picture) II. Title.
PS3569.N88Z465 2010
811'.54—dc22
[B]
2010023904

Cover design by Laura Mazer
Interior design by David Bullen

Printed in the United States of America

COUNTERPOINT
1919 Fifth Street
Berkeley, CA 94710

www.counterpointpress.com

Distributed by Publishers Group West

10 9 8 7 6 5 4 3 2

Contents

| | |

Foreword

WILL HEARST

| | |

The chance to make a film is always a long shot. Unlike a poem, it's a collaborative game. No one person controls all the variables. This is how it happened . . . this time.

In the late '60s while I was still in school, but more interested in sex, travel, and girls than in scholarship, I became interested in the literature of the Beats. This had something to do with California. I was raised in the cold granite corridors of New England, but we spent summers in the West, a sunset land of freedom, possibility, bigger vistas, and hot weather. I wanted to write, live, like Kerouac.

I read *The Dharma Bums*, and I liked that book better than *On the Road*, which is of course Kerouac's masterpiece. I loved the originality, the story, the depiction of that hip Mill Valley scene, and the marvelous language. But one of the things that stood out in that story was the portrait, in a fictional setting, of the character Japhy Ryder. This person who remains at the center of the action is a vivid character with a particularly different and unique point of view. He has his own interior compass, and that character always fascinated me.

By the '70s I discovered the poetry of Gary Snyder, *Rip Rap and Cold Mountain Poems*, and loved it because it had such a feeling of the West. He wasn't a New England academic; there was something fresh and Western about the voice of that poet.

Sometime later, and I don't remember exactly when, I finally uncovered, in a biography or some criticism, that the real poet Gary Snyder was the person on whom the character Japhy Ryder had been based.

I think that was the birth of this project. It became a detective story. How did they connect? As time went by and the Beat Generation began to pass from the scene, it occurred to me that Gary was still practicing, and I became interested to see if he would write for the newspaper. By that time I was the editor and publisher of *The Examiner*, in San Francisco, and we had an Op-Ed page feature, which was a relatively new thing at the time, where we invited people who were not part of the staff of the paper to write essays and editorials and generally nonfiction material.

So we asked Gary if he would be interested, and he sent back this absolutely beautiful essay later republished in his collection, *The Practice of the Wild*. Clearly this man, the Pulitzer Prize–winning poet, could write simply beautiful prose: thoughtful, scientifically grounded, but with a haiku voice.

More time went by, and I met Gary a few times and got to know him, and I continued to believe that he had a wonderful gift with words. He had a clear, unusual mind, and there was something utterly unique about him and his work. And the relationship between the poetry and the poet began to come into focus in my mind. He had a view of the natural world that transcended politics as usual. He was like Japhy Ryder, but he was not Japhy Ryder. Still, I don't think I knew Gary very well.

At another point, working to help found *Outside* magazine, I came to know, distantly, Jim Harrison, who was also a poet but perhaps better known as a novelist. Jim had written a very funny but highly irreverent profile of his fishing trips in Key West. It was so raw I wondered if it could ever be published. My first impression of Jim was that he could not abide any kind of flattery, and he could detect a false note with the precision of a delicate radiometer. Even on the telephone one could hear in his raspy voice and fine diction the influence of poetry.

It was not until after the year 2000, maybe twenty-five years later, that I really got to know Jim and spend time with him. We became friends, and so one day I posed the idea to him, in the form of a question: "Hey, do you think it would make sense to try to make a documentary picture, a kind of profile, of Gary Snyder?" And Jim, to his credit, instantly said, "Yeah, I think that's a great idea, you ought to do it. And in fact, I will help you, I know Gary, and I will talk to him about it, and I will do the interview."

So I thought, *Wow, okay, so a smart writer like Harrison thinks that the idea of doing a documentary on Gary makes sense.* So that gave me some confidence to do more work on the project. But I was slow to pull it together, more time passed, and I remember very distinctly a weekend barbecue with Jim Harrison, and he pulled me aside and said, "Hey, what happened to that Gary Snyder project?" And I said, "Well, I'd still like to do it." And he said, "Why don't you stop liking to do it, and actually do it."

That was the final kick, or spur, to put together a crew, raise money, and talk to Gary more seriously; Jim was an enormous help there.

A documentary is a piece of journalism; you don't go into it with your story already written. You go into it to find out what the story might be. I knew Gary would make a good interview. I also knew he could be quite terse in the way that he spoke. I had no doubt that once we got him going we would find more than enough material; one thing would lead to another. My background convinced me, if you have open access to a subject, you ought to be able to find the story.

But Gary said he didn't want to be interviewed at his house in the foothills; it's been done before. He said, "I'm tired of it, and I don't want to be a Beat poet cliché." Things were stalling, when Jim had an idea. My cousin had done a lot of work to create an agricultural easement at the Piedras Blancas ranch down on the California coast. The net effect was that this land, this very beautiful section of grass and range country at San Simeon, would stay undeveloped in perpetuity.

It also meant that it was going to remain a desolate cattle ranch and was not generally open to the public. So Gary, prompted by Jim, said, "I tell you what: I'll give you the time, and I'll sit and be interviewed, and I'll spend several days with you, but let's shoot it down at the ranch, because I'd like to walk it, and I've never seen it, and I like the Central Coast."

We still had to assemble a crew, to find the right people who had a feeling for the subject. I knew the director should be John J. Healey, who had already made a documentary in Europe about the poet Federico García Lorca.

Casting is time well spent on any project. You have a feeling in advance, because you love the script, or because you believe in the subject, of how the movie will go . . . but something else happens when you start to shoot. The best people bring their A-game. They add to the show. Fresh things begin to happen. The movie starts to unfold itself.

As a producer, you learn the most important thing you then can do is feed everybody, see that they are comfortable, and worry about the cars. As Napoleon Bonaparte observed: "An army marches on its stomach." Think about food, fuel, and transportation.

Finally, when the filming ends, the editor looks at everything you shot and tells you here is the movie you made. It changes again. Music and sound, which seemed so peripheral, begin to shape and cue the action. Your child has begun to walk on her own legs.

So we had a great locale and a commitment to participate. When Jim and Gary got together and started talking, all we really had to do was make good sound and frame the shots. The story of Gary's life and how he came to think the way he does emerged from their conversations.

Like any good profile, like something you might read in *The New Yorker*, you discover so much more when you hear the actual words of the subject, and see the animation in their eyes, than you would ever have learned by merely researching that same subject.

Introduction

JOHN J. HEALEY

| | |

I worked in production in the feature film business as an assistant director for fifteen years before I decided to make documentaries. Taking advantage of the fact that I had a long history with Spain, good relations with the Lorca family, and an important date was approaching, I made my first film in 1998 about the life and work of Spanish poet and playwright Federico García Lorca. It was aired in Europe in June of that year, marking the hundredth anniversary of his birth. One of the people who contributed to the financing of that film was Will Hearst.

Will became friends with Gary Snyder and Jim Harrison when he was still in the magazine and newspaper business, and the idea to do a film on Gary came originally from Jim, I believe. The concept ebbed and flowed over a number of years, and when it reached critical mass Will called and asked me if I'd like to direct it.

I knew Jim Harrison's work because I have been a serious reader of fiction since my teens and Jim's oeuvre held a solid place on my list of favorite contemporary literature. But I knew very little about Gary Snyder. There is some irony in the fact that both of my documentary films to date have had poets as their subject. I myself have never been a great reader of verse.

Will flew Jim Harrison and me to San Francisco in November 2008 so that we could meet and scout locations. Jim had already been working on a list of questions for Gary, and Will and I added some of our own. Jim is an easy man to love. He is very wise and very funny, at ease with his id, and a gentleman. After a long dinner at the Zuni Café, his worries about me, I think, subsided. The opportunity to shoot the film on the Hearst Ranch resonated with me on different levels. I have been a guest there during various phases of my life since I was fourteen, and it is one of my favorite places on this Earth. On that November trip Cynthia Lund and I flew down on a little plane, landing on the ranch's airstrip where I had first learned to drive a stick shift. We were met by Will in his Jeep and by master ranch hand Bill Flemion in his massive pickup. We drove all over the place that day, including to some extraordinary locations that were quite far away and required significant vehicular stamina to reach. In my head I already knew that, barring some compelling reason, we would probably not be able to film at these more distant locations once we had our "cast" and crew assembled. Weather would also be a factor. Driving on the ranch in November was still relatively easy, although Will's Jeep did work itself deep into a mud hole at one point. But generally it rains along the central California coast during December, January, and February, and the shoot was scheduled for the last week of February, so it behooved us to find places we liked that would also allow us to stay relatively close to structures where we could shoot indoors if forced to.

It was during this trip to California that we interviewed potential crew members. We went with Claudia Katayanagi for sound because she has the right level of technical obsession and because she had worked on something with Gary Snyder once before. We chose Robin Lee to edit the film because, in addition to his calm demeanor and enthusiasm for the latest digital editing techniques, to our astonishment he was extremely familiar with Gary's work. We chose Alison Kelly to shoot the film because after interviewing some very competent Bay Area cinematographers with deep documentary experience, she was a breath of fresh air, a woman more at home with independent feature films, who has a great technical competence, a wonderful sense of humor, and a serious commitment to quality. Our mutual respect for Terrence Malick also helped to seal the deal. Before flying back to Spain I went to City Lights with Jim and bought everything Gary had ever published, and before the month had ended I had read it all.

Cut to February 2009: I returned to San Francisco a few weeks before the shoot to review and choose the archival material we would be using. On the way there I stopped in New York to visit the Allen Ginsberg Foundation, located in Ginsberg's last residence in the East Village, where a wonderful collection of photographs is kept.

The weather was not auspicious. It was raining often during the second half of February, and during my drive from San Francisco down to the ranch on the twenty-third it rained on and off. By the time I arrived at San Simeon all the crew were there, most of them up from Los Angeles in two white vans packed to the gills with equipment. After loading everything into a staging room at the bunkhouse, we had a catered dinner together and watched the Academy Awards ceremony on a big flat-screen TV. This was Will's idea, and it was a wonderful way for everyone to break the ice and to start feeling comfortable with each other. We spent the following morning doing a tech scout of the locations, shooting tests, and preparing the room at the bunkhouse where the first interview would take place. I thought it best to do our first day's work in a controlled atmosphere, making things as easy as possible, giving the crew a chance to get used to each other, before going out into the wild with vehicles and steady-cam gear and all of the additional paraphernalia one needs when shooting on the fly and off the grid. I should add that an additional advantage to shooting everything at the ranch was the terrific logistical support we had, the vehicles to get us everywhere, the amazing cooking team flown in for the occasion who spoiled us rotten, and the cocktail hour celebrated on location each afternoon wherever it was we happened to end our day. All of this went seamlessly thanks to the sterling organizational skills of our associate producer, Cynthia Lund.

And so it went. After spending all day on the extensive first interview, we spent the rest of the shoot filming at one location during the morning and at another in the afternoon. The weather gods were with us. With the exception of one somewhat cloudy and blustery day when we filmed the ridge walk, it was all sunshine and glistening green vistas. The crew was wonderful, displaying a professional dedication to getting things right regardless of the hour or distance

to the location. We had the great luxury of working with three cam-
eras, and that required significant preparation each time we changed
setups. But it proved to be a good system. The last thing I wanted
was to have to ask either Gary or Jim to repeat what they had just
said for need of a different camera angle.

Of course, by the time we got to the last day, the whole company
was up to speed, in synch, and working like a Swiss watch. This is
always a cause for some frustration on short shoots. The last thing
we got with Gary and Jim present was the dinner scene that pre-
cluded an official wrap-party dinner. On the following day many
crew members started heading home. But the department heads and
our extra camera operators remained, and it was on this final day
that sound went out to record nature and the camera crew went
hunting for beauty shots on the ranch. Some of the best material
we got and that made it into the final cut was captured during those
last hours.

"Directing" a documentary is not the same as directing a fiction-
based narrative film with actors pretending to be other people. In the
latter case, the director's main job is to make sure the performances
ring true. In the case of a documentary film, you want your main
subjects to be as comfortable and true to themselves as possible—
you want to do all you can to urge them along without getting in
their way. Later, in the editing studio, you get to see all that you have,
and it is there the film begins to take shape.

The two men we see in this film are national treasures, as singular
and talented and American as they come. It was a privilege to get to
know them, to be trusted by them, and to be able to do all I could
to render a final product worthy of them.

||| & |||

THE ETIQUETTE

Gary Snyder, Jim Harrison, and *The Practice of the Wild*

OF FREEDOM

Of animals—free agents, each with its own endowments, living within natural systems.

Of plants—self-propagating, self-maintaining, flourishing in accord with innate qualities.

Of land—a place where the original and potential vegetation and fauna are intact and in full interaction and the landforms are entirely the result of nonhuman forces. Pristine.

Of foodcrops—food supplies made available and sustainable by the natural excess and exuberance of wild plants in their growth and in the production of quantities of fruit or seeds.

Of societies—societies whose order has grown from within and is maintained by the force of consensus and custom rather than explicit legislation. Primary cultures, which consider themselves the original and eternal inhabitants of their territory. Societies which resist economic and political domination by civilization. Societies whose economic system is in a close and sustainable relation to the local ecosystem.

Of individuals—following local custom, style, and etiquette without concern for the standards of the metropolis or nearest trading post. Unintimidated, self-reliant, independent. "Proud and free."

Of behavior—fiercely resisting any oppression, confinement, or exploitation. Far-out, outrageous, "bad," admirable.

Of behavior—artless, free, spontaneous, unconditioned. Expressive, physical, openly sexual, ecstatic.

Gary Snyder, *The Practice of the Wild*,
"The Etiquette of Freedom"

PART ONE

Working Landscapes

Trans-Species Erotics

꽃

Going out—fasting—singing alone—talking across the species boundaries—praying—giving thanks—coming back.

Gary Snyder, *The Practice of the Wild*,
"Survival and Sacrament"

JIM HARRISON: The bishop of Lyon in the eighth century determined that animals couldn't go to heaven, because they didn't contribute to the church—which is ghastly, although at the same time they all decided that hell was a place without birds.

GARY SNYDER: Speaking of birds, you said you went to the Platte River sometimes to watch the sandhill cranes.

JH: Oh sure, and I've seen them dance in these great open areas in Northern Michigan, and they start that dance, it's totally heraldic—

GS: Flutter up, come down, flutter up. —There are Korean folk dances that copy that. They call them crane dances.

JH: It's a small-god thing: poetry's very much involved with the spirits of our imagined deities, which have such a natural place—

GS: Small and drab, even.

. . .

GS: There's a stupa—a big round dome cenotaph memorializing the Buddha—in the city of Katmandu, just on the outskirts. These are found here and there all over East Asia, with a kind of round, soft dome and then a spiral on top, and a railing all around it. People always walk clockwise, sun-wise, circumambulating these stupas, reciting little mantras, and it's all very good for your karma to do that. And these are herders and peasants and lamas and ordinary people going around it, with little candles and oil lamps going twenty-four hours, and lots of horses and yaks being led around as well. Because the view is that there are not too many spiritual exercises that animals can do that will really work for them. But circumambulating stupas is one of them. And so their owners take them around to improve their karma.

JH: The culture that introduced empathy and compassion: that might be what distinguishes us from the nonhuman, but not totally—because I've noticed that, when a dog in a dog family dies, the other animals in the family are really quite distraught and uncomfortable and they keep looking around for the other animal for about a month or so. And then they let go. Do they feel the acute loss that humans do?

My dog Zilpha was distraught this afternoon. I'm not sure why. She was trying to communicate. Now, is that language or an expression of feeling?

GS: We don't know.

JH: Zilpha's brave enough to be a bit of a coward. She once saw a big male javelina, which are dangerous animals to dogs, and she looked up at me and looked at the javelina and started to bristle up, pretending she's going to chase it, but she's just running in place—she hasn't moved an inch. It's really like, "Let me have him! Hold me back!" Very comic, huh?

GS: I love being at that point when I write poems.

JH: Are poems themselves expressions of wildness? Because it seems a poem is an example almost of measured chaos.

GS: You raise the most difficult question of all right there, which is, what is the nature of art in relationship to the wild? It's interesting and complicated.

JH: I think of that extraordinary Shakespeare quote, "We are nature too."

GS: Which is true. But what you have to go after is, what is it that is *not* wild? And start at that end.

People often think of art as being the most highly cultured, the most disciplined, the most organized of human productions, but at the same time that it requires a lot of training, it doesn't happen unless you let the wild in.

I'm reminded of what Robert Duncan said: "To be poetry it has to have both music and magic." And magic is the entry of the wild.

Turn off the calculating mind!

. . .

Life is not just a diurnal property of large interesting vertebrates; it is also nocturnal, anaerobic, cannibalistic, microscopic, digestive, fermentative: cooking away in the warm dark.

Gary Snyder, *The Practice of the Wild,*
"Blue Mountains Constantly Walking"

GS: The little series of poems that I wrote with the title "How Poetry Comes to Me," I wrote them thinking about the ways that I perceive poetry as being *there*, or being accessible, and one particular poem, I think, was "It stays frightened outside the circle of our campfire. I go to meet it at the edge of the light."

JH: Yeah. I go to meet it—

GS: I go to meet it.

JH: It's coming out of the darkness.

GS: But you have to meet it halfway.

JH: And who knows what causes the opening and closing of the door. In terms of poetry you are in the ring of the firelight and you go to meet the arriving poem at the edge of the darkness.

GS: And so the suggestion is that the dark is very rich too.

JH: True—fecund.

GS: That came to me, actually, camping one night in the Northern Sierra. It happened the night that I went up that peak on the boundary line—the Matterhorn.

. . .

Our "soul" is our dream of the other.

Gary Snyder, *The Practice of the Wild*,
"Survival and Sacrament"

GS: I started getting my woods training when I was only six or seven years old, and like you I was going into the thickets and finding ways through the swamps in Washington, and then finding my own campsites, and fixing them up a little bit, and then I would go back to it in order to learn to see where I was and to get around.

JH: Have you ever been lost?

GS: I have been in situations where I didn't know where I was for a while, but I didn't think I was lost. I knew that I would get out of it sooner or later and figure out where I was.

JH: The interesting thing about being lost is, suddenly everything is in question, including your own nature. It's that dramatic.

GS: If you have reached a point where nothing looks familiar and you can't figure out how to reassemble it . . .

JH: I like it.

GS: The only time I have ever been that lost was in the city of Katmandu. I got lost in some back alleys.

JH: I've often thought being lost is like a sesshin when you sit for a long time and then a gong goes off and you get up and the world looks completely different.

GS: Well, that is like enlightenment.

I was hiking in the Sierra high country on scree and talus fields one time, you know, looking at my feet. And I noticed then every rock was different—no two little rocks the same. Maybe there is no identity in the whole universe. No two things are actually totally alike.

Every year, in the fall, a certain small number of ponderosa pines in the forest that surrounds my place start dying of western bark beetle. It's never too many, it's a certain number—but why are they dying and why aren't the others?

JH: One wonders.

GS: It's in their nature. Gradually the ponderosa pines that are resistant to western bark beetles are becoming the established trees of the forest. But genetically there's always going to be a few that are vulnerable. What a curious idea.

JH: Sometimes we as liberal Democrats get discomfited by the inequalities of nature.

GS: Well, to go back for a second to *The Practice of the Wild*—many people, including environmentalists, have not taken well to the distinctions I tried to make there between nature, wild, and wilderness. And I want to say again, the way I want to use the word "nature" would mean the whole physical universe—like in physics. So, not "the outdoors."

JH: Not a dualism.

GS: Nature is what we are in. Now, if you want to try and figure out what is supernatural, you can do that too. But you don't have to.

Then "the wild" really refers to process—a process that has been going on for eons or however long. And finally, "wilderness" is simply topos—it is areas where the process is dominant. Not 100 percent dominant, but a big percentage.

JH: But what you run into, in promoting this schema, is people very much preferring things to be fuzzy.

GS: Well, it is fuzzy. So one of the terms I find myself using more now is the term "working landscapes," to be distinguished from the idea of totally pristine wilderness landscapes. And that's what we have here along the California coast—a lot of working landscapes. The wild works on all scales.

JH: Yeah. Some of the wildest places in England are the old Roman cart trails that have eroded. They're called "hollow ways," twenty feet deep; they've become these preposterously dense thickets.

GS: And that's part of it—the wild can be a wood lot. Even the vacant lot in the city can be wild.

.   .   .

GS: The word "wilderness" is commonly interpreted nowadays by the media and by a lot of environmentalists in terms of the language of the Wilderness Act, which made a particular kind of definition of wilderness that was equable to its use on American public lands. And we realize in hindsight that they went a little too far in declaring that wilderness was totally pristine, showing no sign of the hands of man. It's just language, is all.

When I was younger, working for the Forest Service, we were called on to take out an old sheepherder's structure, dating back to the nineteenth century when the Basques actually drove the sheep into the high country meadows. But, well, you know, this has to be pristine now; we've got to take that shelter down. This is supposed to be pristine and this old shelter looks inappropriate.

But now *that* whole mentality has been reversed, too—now you have to have some different vocabulary, so it's declared of "historical value," and they leave it be. This is an ongoing thing. There are people who say that there have always been human beings around, so therefore nothing is wilderness. But the presence of human beings does not negate wilderness. It's a matter of how much wildness as process is left intact.

WILL HEARST: The Mississippi of the environmental movement, as I understand it, was the Blue Planet movement—here's this whole fragile planet . . . Whereas when I hear you talk, you don't talk so much in these cosmic terms. You talk about nature outside my door, ten feet from where I'm sitting, a mile from my house, and that nature ought to be approached first in this region that is smaller and more local and more human-scaled.

GS: The Blue Planet image came from satellite photography. Stewart Brand picked it up and put it on the cover of the first *Whole Earth Catalog* and said, "Our whole sense of the planet has changed because we now have this picture of the planet Earth from outer space; this is one Earth; this is where we live." And I said to Stewart, "Sure, that's good, but people still don't know or learn much, if that's all you say." People say they love nature.

What they mean is they love what they see with their eyes and smell with their senses: the plant or animal life in their backyard or the nearby creek or down by the park. For exactly those reasons, we might start getting to know our nonhuman neighbors, and it would be a help to understand which direction the water is running and where it might have come from. In other words, what are the lineaments of the place we're in? It's hands-on, ground-based nature learning that you can start teaching in grade school. Why is it that the salmon stocks are declining? You can know this.

The point is, "nature" always happens in a place, and generally, whatever you see and learn, you do so in a small place. You learn the mushroom, you learn the flower, you learn a bird, a slope, a canyon, a gulch, a grove of trees—*as place*. And we all live in a place.

JH: We live in particular.

GS: Even if you're only there for a few months, you're in a place. So why not look around and see where you are?

· · ·

The lessons we learn from the wild become the etiquette of freedom.

Gary Snyder, *The Practice of the Wild*,
"The Etiquette of Freedom"

GS: I don't know if this is true or not—that a hen's nest egg nearing the age at which a chick can peck its way out—that if a hawk's shadow moves over the egg, the little chick inside will tremble.

JH: Ah, the intelligence is there.

GS: It's the sort of intelligence that human beings aren't always willing to acknowledge.

I had always sort of stupidly, ideologically excluded domestic animals from my curiosity, thinking, Oh, that's too bad, they've been taken over by human beings, they've been colonized.

JH: But the colonization was very incomplete.

GS: And an animal is an animal. It's another kind of organism, and it's been fascinating to be with her [Emi] and really be forced to live in a world of nonverbal communication, and then to get better at it—both of us.

JH: I've been around Mexican ravens for seventeen years, and I finally passed muster with them last spring. For a long time they'd hide in the bushes and, you know, ambush my dog—but last spring, they started taking the walk with me. I was now accepted by this clan of ravens. Look how long it took to get there.

GS: So you know what we're talking about again is that human/nonhuman interaction. I have a falconer friend who catches and releases different kinds of raptors. He released a young male goshawk about three years ago, and after a little bit of training the hawk settled into the territory, which is a pine forest. And every morning, when he goes for a walk, the goshawk comes out and flies around above him.

JH: Yeah, paying a leisurely visit. You know, any creature that has an easy time making a living and getting their food, like porpoises or otters—they really spend a great deal of time just screwing around. I remember once after a snowstorm, I went out and tracked the haphazard paths of animals, which were going this way and that for no observable reason.

GS: So fooling around has great survival value, really. Evolution's fueled by fooling around. So don't call all of it intelligent design—some of it's goofy design.

JH: Measured chaos, goofy design—marvelous. Is that why our perceptions are so adventurous? In the springtime where I live, on the U.S.-Mexico border, I might see thirty-four varieties of birds all at once. So how do I look to each of those species of birds?

GS: Okay—

JH: And then you can sense the craziness of the genome, or that each cell of that willow tree has nineteen thousand determinates. In each cell of what that willow tree is, everything becomes vivid, you know? The birds, my brain, the birds looking at me, me looking at the birds. Nature becomes totally holographic that way.

GS: Now you can write haiku.

JH: It just enlarges the conception of life. If you know that a teaspoon of soil has a billion bacteria in it, for example—

GS: So how do we put that into a poem?

Zen and Poetry

❧

The way the self arrays itself is the form of the entire world. Whoever told people that "mind" means thoughts, opinions, ideas, and concepts? Mind means trees, fence posts, tiles, and grasses.

Dōgen Zenji

GARY SNYDER: There's an old Zen anecdote, "Not knowing is best." Daowu asked Shitou: "What's the main point?" Shitou said, "Not knowing is best." Daowu said, "Is there anything more than that?" Shitou said, "The empty sky does not obstruct the flowing clouds."

This is the eastern Taiheiyō: the Eastern Pacific. We are on the edge of the East. So where do we go next? Naturally, we look west, to the East. That's where we go. That's the way I think about it.

Here we're today down on the very edge of the ocean, and this forest is probably to a good extent a nonnative forest—especially the eucalyptus.

. . .

To resolve the dichotomy of the civilized and the wild, we must first resolve to be whole.

Gary Snyder, The Practice of the Wild,
"The Etiquette of Freedom"

GS: Hiking up the Matterhorn once, we had to sleep one night on the trail. It was very cold, so we started a fire. We had a huge boulder behind us that was reflecting heat. And as it got down to below freezing, I could hear animals, maybe deer, moving out in the edge of the darkness, so I walked quietly out farther and farther from the heat and the light, and more and more into the cold and dark. And I knew there were presences . . . and I said, "Oh yeah, this is like art!"

JIM HARRISON: Ah, that's a nice one. A metaphor hits you over the head.

GS: Much like Zen—when you are finally not working at it, it falls into your hand.

"Are you going to try to improve yourself or are you going to let the universe improve you?" Dōgen again.

JH: Yeah, because you open your heart to this country effortlessly at some point. When we finished yesterday walking up the road, it was irresistible. You know what I mean? You couldn't control the opening of your chest cavity. It was there in the landscape.

It was impossible to be here today without thinking of Dōgen talking about mountains and rivers, and I thought of the idea that to study the self is to forget the self, and to forget the self is to become one with the ten thousand things. But you don't become one with the ten thousand things—the ten thousand things become one with you.

GS: Dōgen says, "They are one there. If you think that you're advancing yourself into the world of phenomena, that is delusion. You have to let the world of phenomena come to you." And that might be enlightenment.

And so each one of these huge old coastal live oaks, with their remarkably twisting, turning, tumultuous structure . . . It's one expression of what it's like to live in the wind.

JH: Yeah, it can only come without you stepping on any gas pedal.

GS: Which is a good problem for Zen people anyway.

JH: I was thinking of something you first said to me at Davis, and then I read it somewhere later: that "Zen cuts through every-thing, even its own knife." Nothing escapes.

GS: The second-century AD Indian Buddhist philosopher Nagar-juna founded the dialectics of negativity—the double and quadruple negations. But the Zen people would not want you to read that; they'd say, "Just work on your koan."

Where Zen really cuts through itself is in the territory of effort and noneffort and the debate between the self's power and other powers—between Zen and the Pure Land people who say that the best thing to do is to do nothing to improve yourself. Their criticism of Zen is that Zen people stand in their own way by thinking that they can improve themselves.

And then there is something in China and Japan called Zen sickness. It's when you get too easily comfortable with the fact that everything dies and that everything is impermanent—and it gives you the wrong kind of confidence. You might lose your sensitivity to the suffering of people and animals. I had it for several years when I was younger. I'm only now beginning to realize it.

JH: You know, on that note, I had a fairly remote cabin on Lake Superior for twenty-five years, which I now miss very much, and for a long time I felt that this cabin would strengthen, was strengthening me, for my forays into making a living. But it was just the opposite—the cabin strengthened me for more of the cabin.

GS: There are Tang and Sung dynasty Zen teachers who say, "Don't fall into the dark pit of being too self-satisfied in long hours of meditation. Simple tranquility and simple spiritual confidence are not enough." That was the Rinzai school.

CREW: But I think a lot of Western people say they practice Zen, and I feel that to lose one's sensitivity to the suffering of others is why they are doing it, in a way—as a kind of cushioning device against feeling.

GS: Yeah, there's a koan about that too: about someone who, when his wife died, shrieked with sorrow so loud he could be heard for two miles. And that's the koan. Then this student says, "I thought when you're a Zen person you don't feel like that." And the teacher said, "Try shrieking so that you can be heard for two miles."

. . .

One can be called on not to spare one's very bones in the intensity of effort, but at the same time we must be reminded that the path itself offers no hindrance, and there is a suggestion that the effort itself can lead one astray.

Gary Snyder, *The Practice of the Wild,*
"On the Path, Off the Trail"

JH: D. H. Lawrence said, "The only aristocracy is that of consciousness."

GS: What do you think he meant?

JH: I think he meant that the person who is most conscious lives most intensely—if "intensity" is the real pecking order, since life is so limited in length, as we are both aware of recently . . . That the person who experiences life the most vividly—

GS: The most vividly? I'm not sure I agree with how he meant that, but that's a good question—

JH: Why would you disagree?

GS: Oh, because it's too spectacular, too romantic.

JH: Well, so was he.

GS: Of course. At any rate, you could set that beside an East Asian idea of the aristocracy of consciousness, and a Chinese or Korean idea of that would be much calmer, much cooler. Not like a hard glowing gemlike flame, not like a flaming candle burning out—

JH: That's what Kobun Chino Sensei said; they criticized his friend Deshimaru because he said, "You must pay attention as if you had a fire burning in your hair." And Kobun said, "You must pay attention as if you were drawing a glass of water."

GS: Oh, that's better.

JH: This concept of the divine ordinary—

GS: Exactly. There's two sides of Zen, right there. Deshimaru's statement about hair on fire is something you might say to a koan student. You'd say, "This is in the literature; it's like you had a glowing red iron ball stuck in your throat. And that's how serious you have to be in order to do koan study. But, in the long run, you don't want to burn your tongue off."

JH: It's like René Char says, if you are a poet, all you have to do is be there when the bread comes fresh from the oven.

GS: I like that.

· · ·

The practice is the path.

  Dōgen Zenji

GS: If I disagree with the idea of an aristocracy of consciousness, I also identify with the idea that poetry involves a deep connection with a lot of information. It's wonderful what Confucius said about poetry, third century BC: "Poetry should teach the names of the stars, the names of different plants, how to do agriculture through the seasons, and encourage the pleasure and delight of married people, and respect for elders."

 But it strikes me, what we are talking about is the little historical period that you and I both belong to—when it was more taken for granted that part of the work of a writer was to know a lot, and to have read and explored the literature a lot . . .

JH: I've asked current professors in writing schools what they think of this, and they're not really with me. I said, "You're making them spend too much time reading each other's work," whereas the fundamental duty, it seems to me, is to learn the best in all Western and Eastern literature before you start thinking about or reading each other's work.

GS: You've got to get a classical base, like Pound said; it's important not to start from too narrow a base.

On the other hand, the basic principle of the Yamabushi is, We don't need temples, we don't need halls. "Yamabushi" means "those who sleep in the mountains." The universe, the natural world, the wild is our temple; the sky is our ceiling or dome.

JH: Did they really hang you over a cliff by your feet?

GS: Yes.

JH: Jesus.

GS: That's just part of the beginning initiation ceremony. Hold you by your ankles, way over this cliff. And they say, "You have to answer our questions and tell the truth or we will drop you."

JH: How kind of them.

GS: Then we went on to the top of the mountain, near Mount Ōmine, about six thousand feet. Nice, deep forest all around and a small old temple there, dirt floors, no electricity, the whole thing smelling of wonderful ancient incense, and about twenty guys blowing conches with their amazing outfits on. That was impressive, and it was all still going on in the '60s.

JH: Now, not so much?

GS: I don't know. But now American graduate students write books about them. So that's not a good sign.

JH: Yeah, not a good sign. You know, I used to get irritated with how American culture will take advantage of everything—remember all the ads for, you know, the Zen of Parcheesi, the Zen of sex—

GS: For a while I was annoyed by that. I got over it. I don't even think about it anymore. It's one quality of this society—that its commercialism appropriates anything it can get away with. And so you might as well not give it any feed.

Zen just means meditation. It should go back to that.

JH: Yeah, to the simplest form.

GS: Sitting on a stump.

JH: Yeah, maybe. Or under a stump. Under the stump is quite wonderful.

GS: On a stump in good weather and under it in bad weather.

It's the idea that the mountains and the rivers are your landscape for practice; that you don't need a special architecture.

JH: The natural world was a foundation of Buddhism, of course.

GS: It was part of Buddhism. There's some wonderful natural
imagery in the very early poetry of the nuns and monks in Pali,
the Theravadins, almost vernacular poetry; it's actually full of
nature imagery. But the Tibetan Buddhist style is rather formal:
all of their followers and helpers and defenders, set in elaborate
and formalized mandala-style presentations.

But then in East Asia, starting around the ninth and tenth
centuries, you get these wonderful landscape paintings, many
of them painted by Zen priests. And I suspect this to be the
case, although it just may be my own fancy, that the landscapes in Chinese paintings are the functional equivalent of
the mandalas in Tibetan painting. They are nature mandalas
of mountains and rivers, as done by Zen priests.

JH: I saw some of those years ago, at the Asia Society of New York,
a magnificent show of Chinese screens. Their portrayal of the
natural world was vast and overwhelming, and the people in
them looked sort of silly.

GS: Tiny.

JH: Tiny.

GS: But big enough.

Gary Snyder

❧

The heart of a place is the home, and the heart of the home is the firepit, the hearth. All tentative explorations go outward from there, and it is back to the fireside that elders return.

Gary Snyder, *The Practice of the Wild*,
"The Place, the Region, and the Commons"

GARY SNYDER: I like fallacies, the mistakes that men make.

For seventeen years, I had an open firepit in the center of my house. The smoke was supposed to go out an opening in the gables, but a lot of the time it didn't. I was trying to live like I was in a Japanese farmhouse. I even had a hook for the pot over the firepit. But, you know, it takes a long time to realize certain things, and I realized, yeah, the stovepipe was a good invention. So finally I boarded it over and started living with chairs and a table, like Americans do. It's like a friend of mine who did without electricity for fifteen years, and when he finally connected up to an electric line, he said to me, "You know, I can't even remember why I was against it."

JIM HARRISON: I used to live near a farmer who deeply disagreed with daylight savings, and he wouldn't change his clock. He stayed on what he called God's time. "You have to stand up for your rights," he'd say.

GS: [I feel like that sort of personal decision is still possible,] but I'm still living in a kind of protected enclave of my own culture. It's not taking into account as much as it should, perhaps—the majority culture of the United States. I'm a Californian, and my mother was a Marxist feminist.

WILL HEARST: An orthodox left, red-diaper baby education.

GS: Yeah, except it wasn't doctrinaire in any way, just a set of assumptions about your values.

I was brought up in a strong atheist family. They were Depression-era, grassroots, labor-union-organizing social-ists. My grandfather was IWW. Our neighbors were mostly Swedes, and the Swedes were all pretty far left. All of us were small farmers.

My mother had been brought up fairly strictly in Texas, and I don't know in what, Baptist or Methodist, but she totally turned against it when she was about twelve years old, and then became very self-educated in antireligious rhetoric. So when I became interested in Buddhism, my mother, God bless her, said, "All that navel-gazing isn't going to help the people!" But the one thing she did go along with was what actually drew me to Buddhism in the first place: the ethical questions of other creatures. So since that was a part of it, my mother said, "Well, that's okay." That had her approval.

.   .   .

GS: Buddhism came to me when I was a teenager, living on our family farm north of Seattle, out back in the edge of the cutover land, in the aftermath of the big clear-cut. I was fretting about the condition of nature, and, in a mix perhaps of curiosity and frustration, I had been going to Sunday school a little bit even though my parents did not approve of it. And here is how I got interested in Asia.

I was just a kid growing up on the stump farm in the Depres-sion, back in the woods, and we'd had a heifer on our dairy farm and it had died. And I was really rationalizing, commis-erating, with metaphysical questions about death and animals and humans.

GEN SNYDER: [Laughs] Being a seven-year-old, yeah.

GS: So in Sunday school, I just had to raise the question, "Will I meet my heifer in heaven?" And the Sunday school teacher —he could have finessed his answer, if he had been a more sophisticated theologian—but what he said was, "No, animals don't go to heaven."

JH: Well, I don't want to go there then! I couldn't take it. Most people eat chicken, pork, and beef, and most of them have never hugged a heifer, or known a chicken, or held a piglet, because of their transference from the world to total urbanity. So they don't know what they eat. I mean, my pig, Priscilla, whose belly I tickled and I'm eating her six months later, is a mixed metaphor for a kid.

GS: And I was pretty mixed up by that—questions about our moral engagement with the nonhuman, an engagement that was non-existent in Sunday school, were hitting me very hard at that age. But then, around the same time, I happened to pick up a funny little thirty-five-cent magazine at a newsstand that said Buddhists believe that animals *do* go to heaven, that in Buddhism all different species of beings are considered to have ethical value. And I thought that made sense. So that's when I began to pull away from the Occidental traditions and became on the lookout for more information about Buddhism, which I finally got when I was at Reed College and began to really start reading and studying. I took East Asian history courses and went to museums—particularly critical for me were a set of Chinese landscape scrolls at the Seattle Art Museum. I was realizing that these are heavy-duty civilizations, with tremendous amounts of literacy; but the thought hit me, whether rightly or wrongly, that maybe this is a case of the possibility of being highly civilized—and here's something you probably don't know: as of the year 1800 there were more books in print in Chinese than in all the other languages of the world combined; and, in the eighteenth century, Tokyo was the world's largest city—a case of being highly civilized and also still respecting the nonhuman.

Then I came upon descriptions of Chinese and Japanese Zen Buddhist practice: self-sufficient, partly agricultural, hardy, a lot of working and walking, not a lot of time spent reading a lot of scholarly books but rather delving straight into meditation and straight into dealing with these riddle-like questions and problems called "koans," where the teacher would growl at you and say, "That's wrong!" and then send you back. And I thought, "Oh, that's just right for me." I was really drawn to that kind of practice. It's very close to poetry. One thing about the Zen tradition is, they've always been painters, artists, poets. I felt drawn to that. And the next step was finding out that the training was still available in Japan—Kyoto, particularly. Now, at that time, I couldn't even go to China—it was off-limits to Americans. I also had the impression, as most Westerners did, that Buddhism in China had disappeared, which turned out not to be true. It's all come back.

I made my arrangements and eventually got some help getting to Japan.

. . .

GS: I had been doing graduate studies at Berkeley in classical Chinese and modern Japanese—I don't know what made me think I was going to get anywhere with it, but because I was already doing it, an American woman who lived in Kyoto got word of me from a Fulbright scholar whom she had over for dinner. She contacted me and said, "I'll bring you over here if you want to help me do translation work, and then you can also do Zen study." And that's how it worked out.

So my sponsors in Japan warned the monastery that I was coming, but that didn't mean they knew who I was when I got there. They just thought, "Oh, that's a weird-looking monk."

I was as serious about it as you could expect an American to be, whatever that means. After I'd been there a few days I went over and had tea with the teacher, which is what everybody in Japan always does the first time they do anything: have tea together. And he said, "Well, when your Japanese is better, maybe I'll take you as a student." So that was another seven or eight months. But in the meantime I did a lot of sitting meditation with the monks in the monastery, just quietly sitting there, which is the old tradition in Zen in East Asia: you don't start working on anything in particular for the first year; you just settle into your own reading and into observing your own mind—perfectly good thing to do. I can't believe I had time for it in those days, but I did.

.   .   .

GS: This is the early 1960s, in Kyoto, Japan, when I was a Zen student at the Daitoku-ji Monastery, or *semmon dojo* study hall of the great Daitoku-ji compound of Rinzai Zen temples there. I'll describe my experience as a *koji*, a lay adept, at Daitoku-ji.

We sat cross-legged in meditation a minimum of five hours a day. In the breaks, everyone did physical work: gardening, pickling, firewood cutting, cleaning the baths, taking turns in the kitchen. There were interviews with the teacher, Oda Sesso Roshi, at least twice a day. At that moment, we were expected to make a presentation of our grasp of the koan that had been assigned to us. We were expected to memorize certain sutras and conduct a number of small rituals—daily life proceeded by an etiquette and a vocabulary that were truly archaic. A steady schedule of meditation and work was folded into weekly, monthly, and annual cycles of ceremonies and observations, which went back to Sung dynasty China and, in part, clear back to the India of Shakyamuni's time, the historical Buddha.

Sleep was short, the food was meager, the rooms spare and unheated. But this, in the '60s, was as true in the worker's or farmer's world as it was in the monastery. Novices were told to leave their pasts behind and to become one-pointed and unexceptional in all ways except the intention to enter this narrow gate of concentration on their koan.

We also worked with lay supporters, often farmers, in downright convivial ways. We would stand out back in the vegetable gardens with the locals, discussing everything from new seed species to baseball to funerals. There were weekly begging walks down city streets and country lanes, chanting and pacing along, our faces hidden under a big basket hat, waterproofed and dyed brown with persimmon juice. In fall the community made special begging trips for radishes or rice to country regions three or four hill ranges away.

Begging for support from the community is a Buddhist tradition from the very beginning. The early Buddhist community of monks and nuns went begging every morning, and all the food they ate was obtained by whatever was donated into the bowls they carried. And if they got no food, they went hungry that day. It comes somewhat later, particularly in China, that the monks started settling down and growing their own vegetables.

But begging is still foundational, even in urban Japan. So since special begging trips are out of town, we'd catch a little interurban train. All of the monks get on the electric train and go for thirty-five minutes to a different district—they loved to do that—and then get off the train with their bags and go walking through those villages that were accustomed to seeing monks from Daitoku-ji maybe every year or every other year, or maybe not for five years. But the name of the monastery is written on the bags. So they say, "Oh, the monks from Daitoku-ji are here for rice." And so they would give each one a cup or two, and after a day of this, you've got bags and bags of rice.

· · ·

GS: Back to the spring of 1959 in Kyoto, after a year and a half of living in the Zen world. I decided to take a break, so I took the train up to Yokohama, having heard word of a bar there that also served as an informal hiring hall for American seamen. Go down the length of the bar to the door at the end, open the door and go in, and the second room is a hiring hall. So I did that. And there was a blackboard and couple of people writing and they said, "What do you want?" And I showed them my seaman's papers and I said, "I want a ship." They said, "There's a tanker leaving in forty minutes and they're shorthanded."

So I got on the boat, went down into the engine room, and was told, "Don't do that, don't do that, don't do that, do that, and if you don't do it right, the whole ship will blow up." And then he walked out. It turned out to be nine months before I could get off that ship. It went from Yokohama to Guam to Sri Lanka to the Persian Gulf, to which we made four or five trips for oil and deliveries, then to Samoa and finally back to Long Beach, where they paid us off. I wrote a poem called "Oil" at that time.

And I recall the last time I came back from Japan by ship, which was when I came back with my books and then with my family, in 1968. I woke up early one morning after two weeks, and the sun was rising and I could see some green hills, just off to the port side, and I looked at it again and said, "Oh, that's Stinson Beach." I recognized some of its oak trees. What was waiting for me past those oak trees, of course, was America in the late 1960s.

It would have caused serious culture shock for anybody because America had already changed so much. When I first went to Japan in 1956, it was still the Eisenhower era. And you know, Eisenhower wasn't a bad guy; it's just that the country was still very simple, and straightforward in its sense of superiority and material pride. But when I came back, everything was up in the air.

One of the first things I noticed when I came back was that everybody talked a little bit too fast, and they took too much for granted.

JH: Literary historians of that time were upset because, even though you were such a central figure, you weren't even here. I thought it was comic.

GS: Well, I was a shadow. I was here long enough, and then I got out while I was still ahead.

. . .

GS: I went back to Japan on a visit in about 1975. By then, all the farmers that I had known and all of the rural places I used to roam around in had gone over from small oxen and hand labor to really nifty little bright blue tillers, like Rototillers and little tractors. So I asked them, "How do you feel about using these machines?" And they said, "Well, these are nice."

I think they have more respect for machinery in Asia, and are less troubled by it. I saw, on my visit, a younger man working with one of those machines and getting furious with it; he banged it, swore at it—and an older man beside him said, "Don't swear at the engine, it's got a soul, you know?"

There are some very odd things about Occidental culture that I'm still trying to sort out, and one of them—that I find or, at that time, found in myself—is a kind of resistance to technology, a feeling that machinery is impure. And yet, straight from Kyoto, in the spring of 1959 and in the middle of my Zen training, I willingly attached myself to a gigantic oil-bearing tanker as a seaman.

. . .

WH: Do you remember what your koan was?

GS: There are only three koans that beginners start with. Mine was, "Before your mother and father met, show me your original face. What is your original face?" And my teacher, Oda Sesso, would say, "Don't explain it to me. Don't give me a philosophical interpretation of it. Don't talk about it that way at all. Show it to me."

I worked on another one, too, the *mu* koan. *Mu* means "no" in Japanese. The koan is, a monk asked Zhaozhou, "Does a dog have the Buddha-nature? Does a dog have the capacity to become fully enlightened?" And Zhaozhou said, "No." Now, what *is* that "no"?

WH: So the point is, what's being negated? Is it the question or is it the whole . . . ?

GS: The question is really no—to go past yes or no.
    I've already said too much.

WH: A friend of mine used to joke that a book needed to be published called *A Thousand and One Zen Koans and Their Answers.*

GS: Well, you know, such a book has been published in Japanese. It really does exist. Of course, the Zen masters say, "Oh, that doesn't do any good, because we always know how a person got to that point. Besides, the answers are not the answers. The answers are where you're at."

.   .   .

WH: Can you talk about your time as a merchant seaman?

GS: At the end of my first year in college, a year which I kind of wasted, I knew that my scholarship wasn't going to be renewed because of my feckless behavior. However, one of my friends at Reed said he could get a job with the National Maritime Union in New York City. I thought that was a great idea. It was a great idea. I was only eighteen. So at the end of the year the two of us hitchhiked from Portland to New York City. It took us two weeks because we went out of our way, took our time, and looked around. And besides, this was before the freeways, before the interstates were made. It was just two-lane roads, Highway 40, the old Lincoln Highway, all the way. There were complications in New York because of a maritime strike. But eventually, after a month in Manhattan learning my way around, I got onto a South America–bound ship through the Marine Cooks and Stewards Union, which had a sign on the wall of the hiring hall that said NO RED-BAITING, NO QUEER-BAITING, NO RACE-BAITING. 1947! And a little sign below it that said FIRST OFFENSE — $100 FINE. SECOND OFFENSE — YOU'RE OUT OF THE UNION.

So off I went with the Marine Cooks and Stewards Union, which was probably one-third brown, one-third black, and one-third white. It was great, and I did make some money, more than I had ever made before in such a short time. So then I hitchhiked back to the West Coast, ended up in Los Angeles, hitchhiked back up to Portland, and got back into Reed with my own money. The second year, I did better.

Human Studies

❧

All together elsewhere, vast
Herds of reindeer move across
Miles and miles of golden moss,
Silently and very fast.

W. H. Auden, from "The Fall of Rome"

GARY SNYDER: The nature of language is biological and wild. Our language, or our capacity for language, is more a part of our hard-wired nervous system than it is a part of our culture. We learn the language through the culture that we're in, but the origin is already in us; it always has been.

You know, I'm not a nature writer—but the animal here is reflected.

In North America, animals are more a part of our world, and they remain more a part of our world than in most places. In my world, the Northern Sierra world, there are cougars, there are black bears.

JIM HARRISON: But people just don't accept that all our six hundred grizzlies, for example, are individuals.

GS: And they have feelings.

We are still exploring the territory of knowing animals, and interacting with them. But including them in our dialogue is the new thing.

. . .

Civilization is part of nature—our egos play in the fields of the unconscious—history takes place in the Holocene—human culture is rooted in the primitive and the paleolithic—our body is a vertebrate mammal being—and our souls are out in the wilderness.

Gary Snyder, *The Practice of the Wild*,
"Survival and Sacrament"

GS: In Paleolithic cave paintings, an interesting question is what they chose to represent, and what they chose not to represent. Throughout southwestern European cave art, there are almost no human figures. And whatever human figures are there are just really crude stick figures. But they represent animals beautifully.

And they don't represent all animals. Horses are most represented, cattle or bison or aurochs come a close second. In only a few places, a hyena. So there is some kind of discrimination, some set of choices going on in terms of what is represented.

JH: You rarely see just a complete human being; they're half crane, half man, whatever—the humpbacked flute player, Kokopelli. Or some distortion of the human. Why would that be?

GS: Perhaps they already knew themselves so well, they didn't have to portray or exteriorize themselves. Or, they saw as much of themselves as they wanted to see in animals?

JH: Or, they are painting what they revere and they don't necessarily revere themselves.

GS: Or they do, but they don't have to represent it. In fact there is very little pull to represent the human figure except in ancient Greece and then later in India. But the Chinese never did learn how to draw a human body; the Japanese, just barely. It took the Greeks to really get the body down.

And of course, in the European art tradition, all through its history there are naked bodies. Life studies never stopped. Now, the Chinese would never do that, and still won't—at least not remotely like with the intensity of the dialogue, as in the European heart and mind, between the pagan and the

Judeo-Christian realms. Look at Ovid, the first-century BC Roman poet who was exiled to Albania and there rewrote all of the Greek myths in his *Metamorphoses*. That Latin text became a standard in schools through the Middle Ages and the Renaissance and on into modern times.

So there's this singular body of highly respected pagan lore written in very classy Latin that all schoolchildren read, and then there's the whole Judeo-Christian lineage of music and church and study—these two lines run parallel to each other, and at the same time Europeans can to some extent keep them separate in their hearts and minds through the centuries. It's very interesting.

I have been thinking about Europe lately—it's a fascinating place after years of working with East Asia—its complexity, its diversity, its tribal qualities; and yet, even with all those languages and differences, a distinctive European culture of learning, of music in particular, and finally science in the seventeenth century, emerged with an energy that is really remarkable.

Unfortunately, since the gradual conversion in Europe to Christianity, there has been a steady effort to undermine non-Christian charismatics—generally women, generally village people, people knowledgeable about wild plants.

The Western discipline of anthropology has been battered about a lot—in some cases by its own mistakes, its early assumptions of Euro-American dominance in the world, its assumptions about how you go about getting information. The old model of driving up to some third world village with an interpreter who says a man here is going to pay you to let you talk to him—

JH: It's pretty silly.

GS: But that went on for years, until the rise of ethnic consciousness, minority consciousness—from the 1950s and '60s on, Native Americans and people everywhere became very skeptical of what they called anthropologists. And for good reason—they all had anthropologist horror stories they could tell, including the anthropologists. And all this time I'd been thinking that a lot of anthropology is just the humanities in a bigger sense—a humanities that includes non-European people, noncivilized people, and includes deep history. Prehistory is usually considered something you just don't think about, whereas that's really most of our history.

So, it would be possible, and I would love to see it done, to teach what human beings have been and done on a larger time-scale and on a wider cultural scale, and just call it something like human studies.

JH: Human studies. You know, it's for exactly those reasons that I got interested in a new discipline called human geography. It's fascinating to study why people are where they are, over a sweep of twenty thousand years.

There's the whole concept of geo-piety, what you see in New York, particularly—the old fun about everyone outside of New York City being de facto a regional writer.

GS: That's always amused me, in light of the probability, or the inevitability, that North America will be fifteen or twenty different countries five hundred years from now.

JH: I'm not so sure it isn't now. When I'm in France trying to explain America, I say, "Well, there's basically six countries: South, Southwest, West, Northwest, Midwest, and East."

When I've been on the research hunt, I have mostly questioned why people are where they are. Aside from any academic discipline, form of geography, et cetera, I started talking to people of all ages about where they were. It's a problem, linguistically, to actually know where you are.

GS: It's a neighborly thing.

JH: But you do get disappointed, and I imagine this is because the basic habitat for about half of Americans is television.

GS: Which ain't no habitat.

JH: But that's their frame of reference—pop culture . . .

GS: But when we say "pop culture," I think of two kinds of culture. One is the pop culture that is basically presented by the media, and the other would be genuine popular/populist culture—folk culture, as they used to call it. There's a lot of folk culture out there that's not being portrayed in the media. Living up in the foothills in Nevada County, where people do a lot of hunting, have hunting dogs, are serious about different kinds of fishing, serious about their horses, serious about their dogs—that's not in the pop culture of the media. How many loggers felling trees have you ever seen on TV? It just doesn't happen.

JH: But at the same time, nothing was more ludicrous than when people would proclaim that television has made everyone the same. It hasn't. I'm the one driving around—the media often doesn't get off the freeway, unless there's an explosion of some sort. But you drive around, visiting places, and there are wonderful dominant peculiarities everywhere.

GS: There's a real lust for centralization that is still going on. And the Chinese are totally caught up in it. Chinese national pride is very much based on the idea of China being a large unified country with a five-thousand-year history. Everybody's taught that in the schools.

It's been an icon for China for centuries. And yet, it doesn't quite hold up, in the actual study of history. Edward Reischauer, an impeccable scholar, points out that, yes, some very interesting cultural and technological accomplishments came about during some of the big dynastic periods. But he demonstrates that if you look at the dynastic interim periods, two or three hundred years here, fifty years there, two hundred years here—when there was not a centralized China, but maybe three or four small kingdoms—those interims were usually, he says, the most creative.

JH: I'd started to wonder if that might be comparable to our own oppositions between federalism and state/regional rights . . .

GS: It's more expansive than that. China is actually a very diverse place. They speak seven different languages or more. The only thing that makes it look like they have linguistic unity is the use of the Chinese character, which enables speakers of all of those seven different languages to read the newspaper and pronounce it in their own way. It's worked for centuries.

In the West, of course, what worked for centuries was Latin.

· · ·

Now, [past] the end of the twentieth century, most societies are not even halfway functioning. What does poetry do then? For at least a century and a half, the socially engaged writers of the developed world have taken their role to be one of resistance and subversion. Poetry can disclose the misuse of language by holders of power, it can attack dangerous archetypes employed to oppress, and it can expose the flimsiness of shabby made-up mythologies.

Gary Snyder, A Place in Space,
"What Poetry Did in China"

GS: I haven't become very involved with Tibet but I do feel strongly about it, and I'm so annoyed with the Chinese government that the last three or four invitations I've had to China I had to turn down, because I didn't want to embarrass my sponsors, faultless academics and writers all, because I knew if I got over there, I wouldn't stop myself from criticizing the way China moved into Tibet. For the sake of those who guilelessly would invite me, I've just stayed away.

WILL HEARST: What do you think is going on there? Is it natural resources? Are the Tibetans kind of the Native Americans of China, getting in the way of progress?

GS: Modern Chinese people are educated to believe that Tibet was always a part of China. At U.C. Davis, I had contact with young professors and graduate students from the Chinese mainland, and they'd all say, "Oh, well of course Tibet has always been part of China." So that's what we're up against in terms of the Chinese public, although there's also a Chinese public that's very uncomfortable with the way Tibet has been treated.

Historically, Tibet has always been an independent country with an independent writing system, independent religion, a very different culture that had its own diplomatic connections with China and a lot of interest and respect for China generally, but they've taken as much from India, central Asia, the Himalayas as they have from China.

So what is China doing? They want a place to test nuclear weapons. They're hoping for mineral wealth. They're paranoid about their borders with India and Russia. They want more living space because they think they're too crowded, so they've shipped hundreds of thousands of Han Chinese to Tibet where they think it's too cold and where they're not welcome. This in addition to the serious oppression of the Tibetan Buddhist monk and lama minority who keep speaking out and keep getting arrested. It's a miserable situation. And if Tibet had lots of oil, the U.S. would be right there defending it.

Uighurs, Tibetans, non-Han Chinese like the Miao, the Lolo, the Nosu—these peoples number many millions, and are called minorities. China could just as well be seven or eight nations. Let it go a little bit, and give up the icon of full centralization.

.   .   .

"You mean there's a senator for all this?"

Allen Ginsberg to Gary Snyder, looking west
across Puget Sound to the farther peaks of the
Olympic Mountains, *The Practice of the Wild*,
"The Place, the Region, and the Commons"

GS: We're very accustomed to the term "regionalism"; it's been used in the past as a marker descriptive of ethnic identities, linguistic differences, cultural differences.

Bioregionalism comes into existence through an academic discipline called biogeography. You might think of it as a subset of scientific ecology—looking at the surface of the planet in terms of all its different biological communities, rather than in terms of political, ethnic, linguistic, or otherwise cultural boundaries. Of course, those boundaries are very real, too. But the bioregionalist approach is posited on the idea that the human community is only one of the communities on any given part of the planet, and that the other communities—plant life, animal life, mineral life—inside the landscape with its watershed divisions, its soil types, its annual rainfall, its temperature extremes, all of that constitutes a biome, an ecosystem, or, as they like to say, a natural nation.

It's not surprising that North America is such an inspiration for bioregionalism. In North America we don't have cathedrals and architectural monuments, or huge public works like the Great Wall of China—we have these wilderness areas.

JH: That reminds me—what did Lévi-Strauss say about art? Because of the wild . . .

GS: Yeah, that definitely connects—and I'm sure he was thinking of European culture. He said, "Art is like a wilderness area or a little national park surviving in modern consciousness."

JH: That's an extraordinary statement.

.   .   .

The involuntary quick turn of the head at a shout, the vertigo at looking off a precipice, the heart in the throat in a moment of danger, the catch of the breath, the quiet moments relaxing, staring, reflecting—all universal responses of this mammal body. They can be seen throughout the class. The body does not require the intercession of some conscious intellect to make it breathe, to keep the heart beating. It is to a great extent self-regulating, it is a life of its own. Sensation and perception do not exactly come from outside, and the unremitting thought and image-flow are not exactly inside. The world is our consciousness, and it surrounds us. There are more things in mind, in the imagination, than "you" can keep track of—thoughts, memories, images, angers, delights, rise unbidden. The depths of mind, the unconscious, are our inner wilderness areas, and that is where a bobcat is right now.

Gary Snyder, *The Practice of the Wild,*
"The Etiquette of Freedom"

GS: One thing I've always appreciated in your novels has been the thickets, and the brush fields, and your own explorations of them. And that's instructive to someone like me, a West Coast Cascade and Sierra Mountain person—

JH: Oh?

GS: —who has been maybe overindulged in high spots and long views and charismatic scenery. And so I really appreciate the noncharismatic depth of what you do when you go through the brush and the thickets —which is exactly what I did when I was eight or nine years old, before I discovered the mountains.

JH: The sensation of thickets—I'm wondering if that's almost my own form of reversion to paganism.

GS: The thicket is a good North American form! And biologically apt—the small gods and the birds hang in the brush.

JH: A wild source of dream images. I think it was something you said—that, though our biographies seem to be somewhat similar, it's our dreams and visions that are unique—

GS: That's in a collection of reminiscences by California Indian elders.

JH: Yeah. I had a dream recently; I dreamt my daughter was in trouble. And—I've had a hundred bear dreams, probably—prehistorically, bears would run on their hind legs, running across the Great Plains gobbling buffalo. And I, in my dream, was running as a shovel-nosed bear across the plains to help my daughter. It wasn't a positive dream! And I thought, Jesus, where does this stuff come from? Animals in dreams are soul chasers, they say.

Of course, dreams emerge from the bioregion. People in America don't dream about knights in shining armor.

GS: Well, of course what's interesting is to look at what those differences are.

    The difference between wild mind and cultivated mind is the difference between art and accounting—one is intelligence used for a specific end, to accomplish something, as against intelligence allowed to explore and find surprises.

JH: Almost as play.

GS: You know, David Brower said something interesting to me once. He said that the human species is not a domesticated species; we are a wild species, and the way we know that is that nobody is controlling who mates with whom. No one controls how we breed. It's a completely impulse-driven system, which is the way nature is: impulse and survival.

·   ·   ·

To speak of wilderness is to speak of wholeness. Human beings came out of that wholeness, and to consider the possibility of reactivating membership in the Assembly of All Beings is in no way regressive.

Gary Snyder, *The Practice of the Wild*,
"The Etiquette of Freedom"

JH: The Chippewa-Anishinabes believe that some people do become bears. Five people are sitting together, and then one disappears—he's become a bear.

    I had a problem once: whenever I ate bear, I had bear dreams, and I was talking to a shaman about it—and by the way, I knew this guy for twenty-five years before I learned he was a shaman. He was a land surveyor. And he says to me, "Well, unless you like bear dreams, don't eat any more bear." And he was very sophisticated, he loved Jung's ideas about animals in dreams, but still he just said to me, "So stop eating bear." Wonderful.

GS: You know, I want to say something about this conversation we're having. It's a very North American conversation. This is not something you can talk about in this way anymore in

Europe or Asia, because they are too humanized, too urbanized, too agrarianized; there's not enough habitat, not enough wildlife, not enough people left that are engaged with interacting with other creatures. You'd never hear this conversation in Japan, except maybe in the remote parts of Hokkaido, where people still engage with the brown bears.

It's a good thing that we can still do it here. I'll tell you why. What would be a normal planet would have a lot fewer people and lots more animals. And what we have now is an irregular, abnormal, and dangerous condition.

CREW: Of the human animal?

GS: Of all animals. There are too many human animals, and the habitat and the existence of too many other creatures are endangered, and we all need each other to be together with sanity. It's a matter of planetary sanity.

JH: We now evidently have evidence of a minimum of ninety billion galaxies in the universe—

GS: I haven't heard that figure.

JH: That's fifteen galaxies for each of us on Earth. That's a lot of galaxies, so if there are ninety billion of them, maybe God needed some small gods to help him out.

GS: Or maybe it's all small gods.

· · ·

For those who would see directly into essential nature, the idea of the sacred is a delusion and an obstruction: it diverts us from seeing what is before our eyes: plain thusness. Roots, stems, and branches are all equally scratchy. No hierarchy, no equality. No occult and esoteric, no gifted kids and slow achievers. No wild and tame, no bound or free, no natural and artificial. Each totally its own frail self. Even though connected all which ways; even because connected all which ways.

Gary Snyder, *The Practice of the Wild*,
"Blue Mountains Constantly Walking"

GS: Monotheism has such a big ego. The idea of the sovereign world emperor . . .

JH: Yeah, it's got its own reasons to kill everybody.

GS: I was reading Livy's history of Rome, and then Gibbon's *Decline and Fall* again; over a thousand years of centralization: expansion clear into England, halfway into Germany, clear out into Persia, all across North Africa. The Roman Empire. Everybody came to despise it, all its border dwellers and colonies, and finally the Romans themselves sickened of it. And when it finally went down, the Vandals knocked down the aqueducts so that no water went into Rome anymore anyway.

Nobody ever tried to make Europe into a central nation again except Hitler.

And after that, Europe and especially the Italians became more localized, almost in city-states, and I think maybe that is the real strength of modern Europe. No official religion, no official language, no official way of being . . .

JH: But we're still seeing the horrors of monotheism today—in particular the theological basis of what amounts to land rape: that God told us this was our Earth and in the brief time we are here we can do anything we want to it.

GS: That's one version of it: the Promised Land, the Covenant, from back in Genesis when people could assume that they have a deal, and that the deal gives them a promised land. As it happened, Canaan was already populated, a flourishing civilization, in pre–Old Testament times.

But the Western Hemisphere, North America, was drawn into the rhetoric of the Promised Land in the seventeenth century. And then once the colonial East Coast was established, California became the Promised Land.

Promised Land rhetoric has been justifying expansion and colonization for two thousand years. It's something we ought to pay more attention to now.

The contract is not there. The Covenant was false. And what one has to do is come to terms with the small gods that actually *are* there.

.   .   .

We can begin to imagine, to visualize, the nested hierarchies and webs of the actual nondualistic world.

Gary Snyder, *The Practice of the Wild*,
"Blue Mountains Constantly Walking"

GS: The first Buddhist ethical precept is, "Cause the least possible harm," otherwise known as ahimsa, which was what Gandhi was talking about; he was translating the Sanskrit "ahimsa" into "nonviolence." It literally means "nonharming." It means looking at every situation in terms of the harm that might be involved and to what degree one can pull back from causing it. It's a challenge for individuals but also a challenge for a family or for a clan or for a village if you accept it as a value.

The thing that sets ahimsa apart from the biblical commandment "Thou shalt not kill" is that it applies to all beings, not just human beings. In India, over the centuries, and then in China and Tibet, they never stopped debating, how far does ahimsa reach? And finally some of the Chinese Buddhist monks threw up their hands and said, "Everything—rocks, sand, rivers."

CREW: But still we talk about ourselves in exceptionalist terms. Is that a good perception or a false one? Are we an exceptional animal or are we another animal?

CREW: Well, it's that Buddhist notion: it's both. You can't throw out the uniqueness of our uniqueness.

CREW: So if you had to answer quickly, what would you say are the human characteristics as opposed to the primate characteristics?

CREW: Gary can do this one.

Postscript:
Current Reflections on the Earth

⚜

Whatever sense of ethical responsibility and concern that human beings can muster must be translated from a human-centered consciousness to a natural-systems-wide sense of value . . .

Such an extension of human intellect and sympathy into the nonhuman realms is a charming and mind-bending undertaking. It is also an essential step if we are to have a future worth living.

. . . It is my own sort of crankiness to believe there is still hope.

Gary Snyder, *A Place in Space,*
"Exhortations for Baby Tigers"

JIM HARRISON: America is now 75 percent urban. When I was born, it was the opposite: it was 75 percent rural. My problem as a country lad is, the level of attention I think I need in cities tires me very easily.

GARY SNYDER: And migratory songbirds flock through Central Park in Manhattan, raccoons run along the backstreets at night—so some wild creatures can adapt better than you and I can. Coyotes in Courtland Park, a pair of greens nestling in the high-rises. Some species will move into any city, anytime, if you just give them a chance.

A place exists because of its stories, though most people's approach to connection and information gathering now is via the Internet.

JH: You'd like this quarrel I had with one of my fact checkers—she

says to me, "The town you are talking about doesn't exist."
And I said, "But I've been there," and she says, "I Googled it
and it's not there." I said, "Everything isn't in Google!"

GS: What town was that?

JH: It's a little town in Nebraska, very much there, on the Niobrara
River near the town of Valentine. I thought the Google dispute
so funny that I asked a friend in Valentine to go over to the
place and take a picture of the old post office, which since has
become a dance hall.

·   ·   ·

*People from the high civilizations in particular have elaborate
notions of separateness and difference and dozens of ways to
declare themselves "out of nature." As a kind of game this might
be harmless. (One can imagine the phylum Chordata declaring,
"We are a qualitative leap in evolution representing something
entirely transcendent entering what has hitherto been merely biol-
ogy.") But at the very minimum this call to a special destiny on the
part of human beings can be seen as a case of needlessly multiplying
theories (Occam's razor).*

Gary Snyder, *The Practice of the Wild,*
"Blue Mountains Constantly Walking"

GS: It's quite clear that all of the year-round spring sites on the
Sierra ridge that I live on were Indian settlements. Grinding
stones are around there, and the oaks are bigger. They were
nourished by special treatment—it's quite interesting to see,
and it has taken me years to develop the eye to see that. Some
old Native American, Native Californian women who do basket weaving went out with me in the woods there, and they
were looking through the forest and meadows saying, "We are
responsible for that."

JH: Uh-huh.

GS: Meaning a certain oak grove, meaning a meadow that had lots
of bunches of deer grass growing for basketry. And then they

would look elsewhere in the woods and say, "We didn't touch that."

So the community is the whole neighborhood in which you clench the nonhuman.

When you get a community of a few people who are willing to deal with and are curious about environmental issues, then you have a constituency that will think about whether or not you want to put a parking lot for a mall in a marsh. Otherwise, the Sierra Club, for example, isn't going to get into that. It's just too small for their attention.

JH: The nearness can be lost in the long sweep of concerns.

GS: Exactly.

I have revised my opinion that this whole ranch didn't have enough cows on it. Now I think it has enough cows on it.

. . .

The capitalist world must rediscover its own conscience, now that it has no adversary.

Gary Snyder, *A Place in Space*,
"Exhortations for Baby Tigers"

GS: In the past, most of the developed world's big industrial systems thought that they could write off everything done to the environment as a noncost. That went on for a couple hundred years, and now people are learning that there are bigger and more complex costs that must be incorporated into our economic thinking.

The odd thing right now is, what with the current global recession, a lot of businesses are declaring themselves to be "green" just as a safety measure; people are rushing to hold up the green flag whether they've changed anything or not, whether they even know what that means or not.

People used to say, "I'm going to go talk to the loggers and tell them they shouldn't cut the trees down." But I tell you, they're not the ones to talk to. You've got to go to the top of the chain. Because there is a subset of corporate business that really does face the consumer, and that subset is extraordinarily sensitive to being blamed, to being sued, to being tarred and feathered from a reputation point of view. And that is a place where even small-scale action can have powerful effects.

There are of course different approaches to individual action from that of the West's democratic and post-Enlightenment empowerment of the populace—petitions and canvassing and demonstrating and so on.

I think it's entirely worthy and a great step forward that populations are willing to do that, but it would be false to think that nobody ever did that before the Enlightenment or before the word "democracy." For fifteen thousand years the world has really been a network of villages, over which various kingdoms and nations evolved to do whatever it is they wanted, but the basic work was still taking place on the village level.

WILL HEARST: But now, the machine's become big enough to get even the ocean to talk back and say, "I can't handle this much." It's a very modern phenomenon, in the sense that nature is no longer so much bigger than us that you have to protect yourself from being eaten. Now, it's nature that appears fragile.

GS: Oh, the ocean, it's horrible what's going on in the ocean.

·   ·   ·

We too will be offerings.

Gary Snyder, *The Practice of the Wild*, "Survival and Sacrament"

JH: I'm wondering what you think of reincarnation.

GS: I think it's a charming metaphor. It's an as-if proposition. That's all we can know, anyway.

I got going on a particular idea about reincarnation when I was traveling in India. Say that reincarnation is the world we're in. Okay? Then, how am I different?

JH: Aha.

GS: Aha. It means that I have done everything already—I've had

1940—Fifth-grade class at Lake City Grade School

Harold Snyder, Guernsey Cow "June" and calf,
circa 1937 (Photo by Gary Snyder)

Anthea Snyder and calf, circa 1937 (Photo by Gary Snyder)

Lois Wilkie Snyder, circa 1950

From left: Gary Snyder, Mrs. Kobayashi, Miura Roshi, and unknown
student at Rinko-in (in Shokoku-ji), summer of 1956

Joanne Kyger and Gary Snyder (Photo © Allen Ginsberg/CORBIS)

The house at Yase, northeast of Kyoto, fall 1960

Departing for long walk from Kyoto to the Japan Sea, April 1961
(Photo by Joanne Kyger)

Gary Snyder and Joanne Kyger in Alamora, India, 1962

In India—Allen Ginsberg at a temple in Delhi, 1962

From left: Philip Yampolsky, Gary Snyder, Donna Lebowitch,
Ruth Fuller Sasaki, Miura Isshu Roshi, Vanessa Coward,
Miss Manzōji, Walter Nowick, and Yanagida Seizan
at Ryōsen-an, 1962

Daitoku-ji sodo monks on empatsu (long-distance begging) in Mie
prefecture (Gary Snyder not a regular monk there), 1962

Gary Snyder in Kyoto Garden, 1963
(Photo © Allen Ginsberg/CORBIS)

Allen Ginsberg in the North Cascades, Glacier Peak area, August 1965
(Photo by Gary Snyder)

Masa, Kai, and Gen Snyder, early 1970
(Photo by Gary Snyder)

Allen Ginsberg at Kitkitdizze, summer of 1974

Gary Snyder and Lois Wilkie (Snyder) Hennessy, circa 1986

every possible experience already. I've been every possible form, I've been a woman, I've been a butterfly, I've been a mosquito. So, why be needy? Why be looking for new experiences? Instead, let's settle in and see what we can really think about now. It puts you in a different place.

Reincarnation's charming to think about, and it is very poetic—I like to think of walking the ghost trail, walking the ghost trail in the stars. But I wouldn't count on it.

JH: I love the idea of being a tree that bends and dances in the wind and has nests in it. I just think I would love to be a tree for a hundred thousand years, to live as long as an entire tree family.

But I can't say I'm greatly concerned about death—I expected to be more concerned as I got older, and it hasn't happened.

GS: I have this tendency to think I should get all my affairs in order, that's the main thing.

JH: Well, I did that.

GS: Well, then you're okay.

I'm just waiting until the price of gasoline gets really high and then some future generation up in the Northern Sierra will have horses again.

PART TWO

Transcript of the Film

GARY SNYDER: The wild requires that we learn the terrain, nod to all the plants and animals and birds, ford the streams and cross the ridges and tell a good story when we get back home.

After Work

The shack and a few trees
float in the blowing fog

I pull out your blouse,
warm my cold hands
        on your breasts.
you laugh and shudder
peeling garlic by the
        hot iron stove.
bring in the axe, the rake,
the wood

we'll lean on the wall
against each other
stew simmering on the fire
        as it grows dark
            drinking wine.

.   .   .

JACK SHOEMAKER: It was clear to a lot of us that the legitimate intellectual heirs to the transcendentalists were the new American poets. And Snyder so clearly came from Emerson, Thoreau, Rexroth—the lineage was very clear.

SCOTT SLOVIC: There are so many different phases in his life from his working-class childhood in the Pacific Northwest to his college and graduate school phase, the Bohemian phase of the 1950s, the Zen immersion of the late '50s and 1960s, the rein-habitation phase of the 1970s where he decided to deeply root himself in the foothills of the Sierra Nevada, the academic phase of the 1980s and '90s where he found himself in a position at UC Davis—and he's continually reinvented himself and done so in an imaginative, thoughtful, playful way, and with a sort of seriousness, but not with heaviness—not without humor.

GARY SNYDER: Did I ever tell you what my wife, Carole, said about you?

JIM HARRISON: No.

GARY SNYDER: When she first met you she said, "Is that Jim Harrison?" I said, "Yeah, that's Jim Harrison," as you're walking toward her on the Davis campus. "He wrote *Dalva*?" I said, "Yeah, he's the guy who wrote *Dalva*." And she said, "I can't believe he had such sensitivity to that woman." She thought you were—

JIM HARRISON: A beast.

GARY SNYDER: Well, she just—she thought that you had captured a certain kind of female consciousness like nobody else had. And then seeing you threw her off.

GEN SNYDER: Yeah. It's good for feminists to see that.

WILL HEARST: It made her think twice about that.

JOHN J. HEALEY: That's original perception.

JIM HARRISON: Nineteen years ago, you sent me *The Practice of the Wild* and you said in the inscription, "If anyone understands this stuff, you probably do." Since I've been reading you rather faithfully for forty-three years, you know, since *Riprap and Cold Mountain*, I'm wondering if it hadn't led me to some wrong ideas about you—but I hope that's what we can discover.

GARY SNYDER: I'd like to find that out myself.

JIM HARRISON: Yes, of course.

GARY SNYDER: I was brought up in a strong atheist family.

JIM HARRISON: Oh, how interesting. Were they populists, Wobblies, that sort of thing?

GARY SNYDER: They were Depression-era, grassroots, labor-union-organizing feminists, [and] socialists, and our neighbors were mostly Swedes, and the Swedes were all pretty far left.

JIM HARRISON: Wasn't that a dairy farm your parents had?

GARY SNYDER: Yeah, we had a small farm, a small dairy farm, you know, making do. My mother had been brought up fairly strictly in Texas, as—I don't know what—a Baptist or Methodist, and she totally turned against it when she was about twelve years old and then became very self-educated in antireligious rhetoric and secularism.

JIM HARRISON: What was her reason, do you think, for turning against that?

GARY SNYDER: Oh, because it didn't make any sense. It didn't stand up to intellectual criticism and she didn't like it. And when I became interested in Buddhism, my mother, God bless her, said, "All that navel-gazing isn't gonna help the people."

JIM HARRISON: That's wonderful: the people.

. . .

JIM HARRISON: In your early poetry particularly, the poetry comes out of the essential near-wildness of your work, you know, and the rhythm of work like *Riprap*.

GARY SNYDER: Part of it was the work and part of it was, I was really caught up at that time in looking for the simplicity of the— what simplicity I could find in the English language. I'd been studying classical Chinese in the graduate school of Berkeley. Literary Chinese is strongly monosyllabic, and so I thought, well, pre-Norman English—the Germanic lineage of the English language—has a lot of monosyllables. And monosyllables are like rocks, you know, and I was used to working with these rocks, and I thought, Well, let me—I'm gonna try to work with monosyllabic English, with an old-style vocabulary like I was building a little rock trail.

The poems I'm going to read from this book were written after I had been working for the Park Service on a trail crew in the high country of Yosemite National Park.

Hay for the Horses

He had driven half the night
From far down San Joaquin
Through Mariposa, up the
Dangerous mountain roads,
And pulled in at eight a.m.
With his big truckload of hay
    behind the barn.
With winch and ropes and hooks
We stacked the bales up clean
To splintery redwood rafters
High in the dark, flecks of alfalfa
Whirling through shingle-cracks of light,
Itch of haydust in the
    sweaty shirt and shoes.
At lunchtime under Black oak
Out in the hot corral,
—The old mare nosing lunchpails,
Grasshoppers crackling in the weeds—"I'm
    sixty-eight," he said,
"I first bucked hay when I was seventeen.
I thought, that day I started,
I sure would hate to do this all my life.
And dammit, that's just what
I've gone and done."

.   .   .

JIM HARRISON: I'm wondering if you could recite that poem you read to your students, you know, how a poem comes.

GARY SNYDER: I could recite it but I would probably change it; that doesn't matter though.

JIM HARRISON: No, no.

GARY SNYDER: That was one of a series of little poems I wrote with the title "How Poetry Comes to Me."

JIM HARRISON: Yeah.

GARY SNYDER: Thinking about the ways that I perceive it as being there or as being accessible, and that particular little poem was, I think, "It stays frightened outside the circle of our campfire. I go to meet it at the edge of the light."

JIM HARRISON: You are in the ring of the firelight and you go to meet the arriving poem at the edge of darkness.

GARY SNYDER: And so the suggestion is that the dark is very rich too.

JIM HARRISON: True, fecund.

GARY SNYDER: And that came to me, actually, camping one night in the Northern Sierra, and it actually happened the night that I went up that peak on the Northern Sierra boundary line, the Matterhorn, with Jack Kerouac.

JIM HARRISON: Oh goodness.

GARY SNYDER: Yeah.

JIM HARRISON: On your camping trip, that—

GARY SNYDER: We had to sleep one night on the trail so it was very cold. We started a fire; we had a huge boulder behind us that was reflecting heat onto us too.

JIM HARRISON: That's nice.

GARY SNYDER: And as it got down below freezing, I could hear animals or something, maybe deer, moving out in the edge of the darkness there. And so I walked step-by-step quietly out farther and farther from the heat and the light and more and more into the cold and the dark and I knew there were presences. And I said, "Oh yeah, this is like art!"

JIM HARRISON: Yes. Oh goodness, yeah, that's nice when a metaphor hits you over the head.

GARY SNYDER: Yeah, yeah.

JIM HARRISON: You know, I was thinking about that because I read that book *The Dharma Bums*, and I was wondering, how long was that actual trip in days, a couple of days or—?

GARY SNYDER: No, just two nights.

JIM HARRISON: Isn't it amazing because—well, that's what novelists do.

GARY SNYDER: Up one night to the summit, back down to camp again second night, back to the car.

Mid-August at Sourdough Mountain Lookout

Down valley a smoke haze
Three days heat, after five days rain
Pitch glows on the fir-cones
Across rocks and meadows
Swarms of new flies.

I cannot remember things I once read
A few friends, but they are in cities.
Drinking cold snow-water from a tin cup
Looking down for miles
Through high still air.

. . .

MICHAEL MCCLURE: At the Six Gallery reading, Allen Ginsberg read "Howl," a very famous poem. It's probably the most popular poem in the world today and it was—all of the things that it protested against are absolutely real, at the same time—and it caused a lot of stir in the press and it caused a lot of stir in the public. That same evening, Gary Snyder read his very deep and important poem—it was the first poem of Deep Ecology I ever heard; as a matter of fact, as far as I know, it was read before the term "Deep Ecology" was generally used, if used at all—and in that audience, many of the people who were terribly moved by "Howl" were even more moved by "A Berry Feast" by Gary Snyder.

. . .

REEL VOICEOVER: *Gary Snyder is another poet identified with the Pacific Northwest, San Francisco, and Reed College. Snyder now lives in Kyoto, Japan, where he's a student of Zen. But for part of 1965, he was a lecturer in the English Department of the University of California at Berkeley. When asked to ad-lib a biography, he gave his usual direct answer.*

GARY SNYDER: *Well, I'd have to tell the truth. I was born in San Francisco, and at a very early age I was moved to Seattle where I grew up on a small farm just north of Seattle. Later, about twelve, we moved to Portland, Oregon. I went to college in Portland, Oregon, graduated from Reed College, spent a little time in Indiana University, and then came back to the Bay Area. I went here to Berkeley in the Oriental Languages Department for about three years, and then for the last eight years I've almost constantly been living in Japan.*

. . .

JIM HARRISON: This guy says to me—we're swimming in a cenote near the ocean, those jungle pools that well up—he said, "Look, if an anaconda comes up to you, don't worry, because he'll catch your scent and turn away." And I said, "Do you mind if I just go to the bar? I'm not . . . quite ready for . . ." I saw them in the zoo in Valladolid, you know, their heads are this big; I don't need an anaconda swimming up to me.

GARY SNYDER: Well, you know, there is a stupa, a big round dome cenotaph memorializing the Buddha in the city of Katmandu, just on the outskirts. These are found here and there all over East Asia with a kind of a round, soft dome and then a spiral on top—

WILL HEARST: Yeah, yeah, you can see the shape.

GARY SNYDER: —railing all around it, you know. So when you go there in Katmandu, people always go clockwise, sun-wise, circumambulating east, reciting little mantras, and it's all very, very good for your karma to do that. And these are herders and peasants and lamas and ordinary laypeople going around it, little light candles, oil lamps going twenty-four hours, and lots of horses and yaks being led around as well.

JIM HARRISON: To get the spirit to—

GARY SNYDER: Because the view is that there are not too many spiritual exercises that animals can do that'll really work for them, but circumambulating stupas is one of them.

JIM HARRISON: I love that.

GARY SNYDER: And so their owners take them around to improve their karma.

WILL HEARST: Why did you get on to that so early in your life? Because even when you were a college student, you were reading Chinese.

GARY SNYDER: You know, I got interested in Asia for the wrong reasons.

JIM HARRISON: Were you attracted to the women?

JOHN J. HEALEY: This could get interesting, yeah.

GARY SNYDER: I was just a little kid growing up on a stump farm in the Depression back in the woods and I was offended by my Lutheran Sunday school teacher.

WILL HEARST: Now, that's the beginning of a story, not the end.

LISA NEINCHEL: Yeah, I was going to say.

GARY SNYDER: Well, I was offended because we had a heifer on our dairy farm and it had died and I was really wrestling with metaphysical questions about death and animals and humans—

GEN SNYDER: Being a seven-year-old.

GARY SNYDER: Yeah, so in Sunday school, I just had to raise the question, "Will I meet my heifer in heaven?"

JOHN J. HEALEY: That's so adorable.

JIM HARRISON: Yeah.

LISA NEINCHEL: Yeah.

GARY SNYDER: And the Sunday school teacher, you know, could have finessed the answer—

WILL HEARST: Yeah, right.

GARY SNYDER: —if he had been a more sophisticated theologian— but what he said was, "No, animals don't go to heaven."

JIM HARRISON: Well, then I don't want to go there!

GARY SNYDER: That's exactly what I said!

JIM HARRISON: I couldn't take—

GARY SNYDER: Our moral engagement with the nonhuman hit me very hard at that age and so that was the first thing to generate a certain interest in East Asia. So then later, I was seeing Chinese landscape scrolls at the Seattle Art Museum, and then I was taking East Asian history courses. And of course, I realized then these are heavy-duty civilizations with tremendous amounts of literacy—but the thought hit me, whether rightly or wrongly, that maybe this is a case of the possibility of being highly civilized and also still respecting the nonhuman.

· · ·

GARY SNYDER: Well, here we are.

JIM HARRISON: Yes.

GARY SNYDER: Another great drainage.

JIM HARRISON: A lot of country here. I know I'm not on the Upper East Side of New York, conclusively.

GARY SNYDER: My second wife, Joanne Kyger, when she came to Kyoto and she and I were talking about Buddhist practice, asked me, "Well, what will happen if I do Buddhist practice?" I said, "Well, maybe you'll lose yourself."

JIM HARRISON: Yeah.

GARY SNYDER: And she said, "Why would I want to do that? I just finally got a self!"

JIM HARRISON: That's right.

· · ·

JOANNE KYGER: Snyder left in February of '59 and I joined him a year later. I'd run up a big bill at Macy's. I was living on my own in North Beach, and he said, "Well, you can come after you pay off your debt" which was $1,000. So I went and lived at this place called the East-West House. That was one of the first communal houses, and it was for people who wanted to get ready to go to Japan.

· · ·

JIM HARRISON: Did they really hang you over a cliff by your feet?

GARY SNYDER: Yeah.

JIM HARRISON: Jesus.

GARY SNYDER: That's just part of a beginning initiation ceremony.

JIM HARRISON: Just hold you by your ankles?

GARY SNYDER: Hold you by your ankles, yeah. They'll hold you way over this cliff.

JIM HARRISON: I don't care for that. I'm vertiginous.

GARY SNYDER: And then they say, "You have to answer our questions and tell the truth or we'll drop you."

JIM HARRISON: How kind of them.

JOANNE KYGER: When I arrived, I somehow weirdly thought I was going to look out on a nation of pagodas. I said, "This looks just like San Francisco."

GARY SNYDER: We sat cross-legged in meditation a minimum of five hours a day. In the breaks, everyone did physical work—gardening, pickling, firewood cutting, cleaning the baths, taking turns in the kitchen. There were interviews with the teacher at least twice a day.

JIM HARRISON: I've thought—in my nickel-ante satoris, I call them—that often, it comes from no effort, you know. It's a realization—

GARY SNYDER: Yeah, finally—

JIM HARRISON: —emerging, well, finally. I suppose that it's fine.

GARY SNYDER: Yeah. When you're not really finally working at it, it falls into your hand.

. . .

GARY SNYDER: Sleep was short, the food was meager, the rooms sparse and unheated, but this was in the '60s, and it was as true in the worker's or farmer's world as it was in the monastery.

    The Zen knife cuts itself—

JIM HARRISON: Yeah.

GARY SNYDER: —the old head monk at the Zen village, Shokoku-ji, said at a *sesshin* one year. He said the perfect way is without difficulty. Strive hard!

JIM HARRISON: [Laughs]

GARY SNYDER: I carried that around with me for years—and I still do, because both sides of it are true.

Novices were told to leave their pasts behind them and to become one-pointed and unexceptional in all ways except the intention to enter the narrow gate of concentration on their koan.

JIM HARRISON: When my brother—who sort of became my father because my father died when I was a directionless twenty-year-old—when my brother died several years ago, it was strange... I couldn't endure any reading, except Hakuin. It was so hard.

GARY SNYDER: Oh God.

JIM HARRISON: You know, there's nothing—in the experience of his death, there was nothing ameliorating. I suppose you felt that way about Carole.

GARY SNYDER: I stayed home and didn't see people for three months, and it wasn't, you know, that I wanted to—I don't know what it was. I just didn't feel like seeing anybody, you know. I wanted to feel things through and think things through. And it wasn't even like suffering; it was like, this bears real reflection.

JIM HARRISON: Uh-huh.

GARY SNYDER: Yeah. I got a poem I want to read you about that.

JIM HARRISON: Yeah, I'd like that.

GARY SNYDER: But I'm not gonna show anybody else, only one or two people.

· · ·

Oil

soft rainsqualls on the swells
south of the Bonins, late at night. Light
from the empty mess-hall
throws back bulky shadows

of winch and fairlead
over the slanting fantail where I stand.

but for men on watch in the engine room,
the man at the wheel, the lookout in the bow,
the crew sleeps. in cots on deck
or narrow iron bunks down drumming
passageways below.

the ship burns with a furnace heart
steam veins and copper nerves
quivers and slightly twists and always goes—
easy roll of the hull and deep
vibration of the turbines underfoot.

bearing what all these
crazed, hooked nations need:
steel plates and
long injections of pure oil.

. . .

JIM HARRISON: Another thing I was wondering about—because I
    read so many opposing views—just what you think of the idea
    of reincarnation.
GARY SNYDER: Oh, boy. I think it's a charming metaphor. It's an as-if
    proposition because that's all we can know anyway.
JIM HARRISON: True.
GARY SNYDER: What I like to do is—I got going on this idea when
    I was traveling and living in India—
JIM HARRISON: Yeah.
GARY SNYDER: Let's say reincarnation is the world we're in—then,
    how am I different?
JIM HARRISON: Aha.
GARY SNYDER: Aha! It means that I have done everything already.
    I've had every possible experience already. I've been in every

Gary Snyder with crew

Gary Snyder

Jim Harrison

Gary Snyder and Jim Harrison with crew

From left: Will Hearst, Gary Snyder, Lisa Neinchel, Gen Snyder, Jim Harrison, and John J. Healey

Will Hearst and Gary Snyder

Gen Snyder, Jim Harrison, and John J. Healey

Gary Snyder

Gary Snyder and Jim Harrison

Gary Snyder, Emi, and Jim Harrison

San Simeon Ranch

San Simeon Ranch

Emi, Jim Harrison, and Gary Snyder

From left: Will Hearst, Jim Harrison, Emi, and Gary Snyder

Emi, Gary Snyder, and Jim Harrison

Jack Shoemaker

Joanne Kyger

Michael McClure

Scott Slovic

Gary Snyder

possible form. I've been a woman; I've been this; I've been a butterfly; I've been a mosquito.

JIM HARRISON: A tree; I like the idea of being a tree.

GARY SNYDER: Yeah. And so, why be needy, why be looking for new experiences?

JIM HARRISON: Aha, truly.

GARY SNYDER: Let's settle in and see what we can really think about now.

JIM HARRISON: Aha, true.

GARY SNYDER: It puts you in a different place.

. . .

JACK SHOEMAKER: There's been a kind of back-and-forth between the counterculture people from this country and some people in Japan, so he's heard of stuff going on, and when he comes back here, he's immediately plugged into the Golden Gate Park Be-In. He's immediately part of the *San Francisco Oracle* culture. When they published the big photograph of the gurus of the counterculture, it's Tim Leary, Gary Snyder, and Allen Ginsberg. It's as if he's never been gone. He even has the right clothes, remember. Even he's dressing like a hippie even though he's come from Japan.

. . .

JIM HARRISON: I've read that fascinating correspondence you had with Allen Ginsberg, and I saw two things in there. I know you go out in public a reasonable amount, but he never stopped going out in public at all, did he?

GARY SNYDER: He lived a public life.

JIM HARRISON: Yeah, totally.

GARY SNYDER: Virtually, yeah, and really quite at home in it.

JIM HARRISON: But you said then some people are very comfortable going in that and others of us aren't. You know, I can hardly bear to do it at all anymore.

GARY SNYDER: Public life is like riding the subways in Tokyo.

JIM HARRISON: Yeah.

GARY SNYDER: You dread it as you approach it. The closer and closer you get to it, the more you dread it, till you actually go through the door and you get in the subway and ride and then it's fine.

JIM HARRISON: It's okay. I dreaded book tours so much that it was more unpleasant to dread them than to actually do them.

GARY SNYDER: Yeah. But Allen, you know, he followed a course of being a public figure, a public intellectual, a public gadfly and researcher and supporter of certain values like the legalization of drugs and opposition to war, and he never let up.

JIM HARRISON: So you don't feel, inside yourself, that there's any kind of war between the public and private world?

GARY SNYDER: I don't do as much public as Allen ever did. And when I was traveling around with Allen many years ago, I would have to stay at my pace, which meant some days Allen would say, "Today let's go there," and I'd say, "You go; I'm gonna stay here today and collect my wits"—

JIM HARRISON: Yeah, truly.

GARY SNYDER: —which I always enjoyed doing, you know, take a day off and meditate and catch up in my notebook.

JIM HARRISON: Yeah, truly.

GARY SNYDER: I don't know when Allen ever had time to do that.

· · ·

JOANNE KYGER: I believe Gary does not like to be called a Beat generation poet because it's become such a limiting cultural catchall.

MICHAEL MCCLURE: Many of the positive things that the Beats practiced have swelled into the general culture in a way that is not seen. They're just—they're there. I noticed twenty or thirty years ago when somebody asked me, "Whatever happened to the Beats; whatever happened to you guys, anyway?" And I said, "You're standing in front of me, kid; you're not calling me Mister, you've got long hair, you're wearing Levi's, you don't believe in war, you idealize the female consciousness as well as the male, you are for the preservation of the planet—and there you are. Don't ask me where they went."

GARY SNYDER: For those who would see directly into essential nature, the idea of the sacred is a delusion and an obstruction. Not only plum blossoms and clouds or lectures and *rōshis*, but chisels, bent nails, wheelbarrows, and squeaky doors are all teaching the truth of the way things are.

JACK SHOEMAKER: I think it always made Gary nervous, the potential—we wouldn't have then called it celebrityhood—but the celebrity culture, the hollowness of it, the temporary nature of it, always troubled him. And remember when he comes back to this country, finally, he buys a piece of property in the foothills of the Sierra and stays in town only for about six months before he goes up and begins to build a house at Kitkitdizze, in a place with no electricity, no telephone, no access, and a very out-of-the-way homestead that he's bought with Dick Baker and Ginsberg, and he's the only one that goes directly up there and starts building.

SCOTT SLOVIC: Gary, through his years of prolonged inhabitation of the western slope of the Sierra Nevada and his conscious reinhabitory efforts to live responsibly in this place as if he were going to be there for thousands of years, as he sometimes puts it, has been able to really know that place and to reach toward the idea of bioregionalism.

JOANNE KYGER: I think he wanted to get more into Japanese life and the Japanese farmhouse with its open hearth in the center really suited him. He later built one up in Kitkitdizze.

GARY SNYDER:

For the Children

The rising hills, the slopes,
of statistics
lie before us.
the steep climb

of everything, going up,
up, as we all
go down.

In the next century
or the one beyond that,
they say,
are valleys, pastures,
we can meet there in peace
if we make it.

To climb these coming crests
one word to you, to
you and your children:

stay together
learn the flowers
go light

.   .   .

JIM HARRISON: Oh, you would like this quarrel I had with one of
my copy editors and fact checkers: she said to me, "The town
you're talking about doesn't exist." And I said, "But I've been
there." And she says, "I Googled it and it's not there." And I
said, "Everything isn't—

GARY SNYDER: In Google.

JIM HARRISON: —you know, "in Google"—including the content
of libraries.

GARY SNYDER: What town was that?

JIM HARRISON: It's a little town in Nebraska on the Niobrara River.
I selected the area because . . . the last of the battles of cultures,
the Lakota struggles, took place in that region. And that was
amazing because we moved them three times. What did Philip
Sheridan say, the old warmonger? He admitted that an Indian

reservation is usually a worthless piece of land surrounded by scoundrels. That's what he said.

GARY SNYDER: I don't know why we're laughing. It's still such a—

JIM HARRISON: No, it's such a preposterously dark period.

GARY SNYDER: You know, to go back a bit for a second to *The Practice of the Wild*, I find that it's hard to—people, including environmentalists, have not taken well to the distinctions I tried to make there between nature, the wild, and wilderness. You know, I want to say again, the way I want to use the word "nature" would mean the whole physical universe.

JIM HARRISON: Truly.

GARY SNYDER: Yeah, like in physics.

JIM HARRISON: Yeah, right, exactly.

GARY SNYDER: So not the outdoors.

JIM HARRISON: No. That's a false dichotomy—

GARY SNYDER: Yeah.

JIM HARRISON: —or a dualism.

GARY SNYDER: Yeah. Nature is what we're in. If you want to try to figure out what's supernatural, you can do that, too.

JIM HARRISON: Uh-huh.

GARY SNYDER: But you don't have to. And then the wild really simply refers to process, a process that's been going on. And wilderness is simply topos—it's areas where the process is dominant.

· · ·

SCOTT SLOVIC: Bioregionalism is a social movement that emerged in the American West in the 1970s. And basically, it describes a type of political orientation that is local rather than global, that is nearby rather than far away. It's based on the premise that if people pay attention to where they are and think responsibly about their interactions with the local environment and with the local human community, they can do a better job—they are likely to do a better job managing their own affairs and their interactions with the natural environment than people who are located far away and who are less invested in that place.

. . .

GARY SNYDER: You know, I just wanted to interrupt to say something about all this conversation. It's a really North American conversation, okay? This is not something you can talk about in this way anymore in Europe or Asia.

GEN SNYDER: Well, I don't know. Maybe among hippies or—I don't know.

WILL HEARST: What do you mean?

GARY SNYDER: Because Europe and Asia are too humanized. Their populations are too large—

WILL HEARST: Too urbanized.

GARY SNYDER: Too urbanized, too agrarianized, so that—

JIM HARRISON: Interesting.

GARY SNYDER: —so that there are not enough—there's not enough habitat, there's not enough wildlife, there are not enough people left that are engaged with interacting with other creatures in those parts of the world. You would never hear this conversation in Japan except maybe in the remote parts of Hokkaido where people engage with the brown bears up there.

GEN SNYDER: Well, you know—

JOHN J. HEALEY: And is that a good thing or a bad thing? Does that have any—

GARY SNYDER: Yeah, it's a good thing that we could just still do it here.

JOHN J. HEALEY: Okay, because—

GARY SNYDER: And I'll tell you why. What would be a normal planet would have a lot fewer people and lots more animals, and what we have now is an irregular, abnormal, and dangerous condition.

JOHN J. HEALEY: Of the human animal?

GARY SNYDER: Of all animals.

JOHN J. HEALEY: Okay. There are too many human animals.

LISA NEINCHEL: Too many humans.

GARY SNYDER: There are too many human animals and their habitat, and the existence of too many other creatures is endangered, and we all need each other to be together with sanity. It's a matter of planetary sanity.

JOHN J. HEALEY: Balance.

GARY SNYDER: Nature always happens in a place.

JIM HARRISON: Yeah, truly.

GARY SNYDER: Nature happens in a place, and generally whatever you see and learn you learn in a small place.

JIM HARRISON: Yeah.

GARY SNYDER: You learn a mushroom, you learn a flower, you learn a bird, you learn a slope, a canyon, a gulch, a grove of trees, a stand of trees—*as place*. And we all live in a place.

JIM HARRISON: Truly. We live in particular.

GARY SNYDER: Even if you're only there for a few months, you're in a place—so why not look around and see where you are?

. . .

MICHAEL MCCLURE: Gary's poetry is an infusion into our culture that's not sufficiently recognized for the power and the depth and the spread of it. Introducing, for example, the term "Turtle Island" to the country. Wow, that's cool!

JACK SHOEMAKER: *Turtle Island* was a book that in its time sold one hundred thousand copies and was a hugely influential book in the environmental movement, in the Buddhist movement, in the Native American movement, in the reinhabitation movement, in the bioregional movement, in the poetry movement. It was a book that won the Pulitzer, won—not the National Book Critics Circle but another major prize. It was and is a hugely influential book.

For All

Ah to be alive
  on a mid-September morn
  fording a stream
  barefoot, pants rolled up,
  holding boots, pack on,
  sunshine, ice in the shallows,
  northern rockies.

Rustle and shimmer of icy creek waters
stones turn underfoot, small and hard as toes
  cold nose dripping
  singing inside
  creek music, heart music,
  smell of sun on gravel.

I pledge allegiance

I pledge allegiance to the soil
  of Turtle Island,
and to the beings who thereon dwell
  one ecosystem
  in diversity
  under the sun
With joyful interpenetration for all.

·   ·   ·

GARY SNYDER: There won't be white men one thousand years from now. There won't be white men fifty years from now, quite; the whole society is going someplace else. I feel that this is one of the most exciting works of poetry right now: it's to capture and make contact with those areas of the unconscious that belong to the whole American continent, the nonwhite world, the world of mythology and intuitive insight that belongs with primitive cultures and ultimately getting back in touch not only with ourselves but with the natural world, with nature, which we've been out of contact with for so long that we've almost destroyed the planet.

Life in the world is not just eating berries in the sunlight. I like to imagine a depth ecology that would go to the dark side of nature, the ball of crunched bones in a scat, the feathers in the snow, the tales of insatiable appetite. It is also nocturnal, anaerobic, cannibalistic, microscopic, digestive, fermentative, cooking away in the warm dark.

LISA NEINCHEL: You guys mentioned reincarnation earlier. I'm just wondering, do you actually believe in it then or you just think the idea is nice?

JIM HARRISON: Metaphor.

GARY SNYDER: It's charming to think about.

LISA NEINCHEL: Yeah.

GARY SNYDER: Yeah, and it's very poetic—I like to think of walking the ghost trail, walking the ghost trail in the stars. I wouldn't count on it.

JIM HARRISON: I like the idea of being a tree, a tree that bends and dances in the wind and stuff like that, and has nests, bird nests in it. I just think I would love to be a tree for one hundred thousand years.

WILL HEARST: Trees don't live that long, Jim.

JIM HARRISON: No, but a tree through generations.

GARY SNYDER: Oh, but a tree family does.

JIM HARRISON: A tree family.

WILL HEARST: You'd like to be a species rather than—

JIM HARRISON: But the idea of coming back . . .

. . .

JACK SHOEMAKER: Gary is remarkable because Gary is seventy-nine years old and still he can wear you out hiking, he can put away a lot of wood, he can handle a lot of work around the place. He complains that he's slowing down a little bit but I

sure can't see it. But above all else, he remains intensely curious, so he's very much involved with the work of a few friends,
and he tries to stay on top of their interests as well as his own.
He's that kind of person. He'll go to Alaska, and all of a sudden
what he wants to find out is, what is it about halibut fishermen?
Who are these guys, what do they do? So he's always filled with
enthusiasms and I think that's the secret of a long life, if you
can remain enthusiastic and curious.

. . .

Waiting for a Ride

Standing at the baggage passing time:
Austin Texas airport—my ride hasn't come yet.
My former wife is making websites from her home,
one son's seldom seen,
the other one and his wife have a boy and girl of their own.
My wife and stepdaughter are spending weekdays in town
so she can get to high school.
My mother ninety-six still lives alone and she's in town too,
always gets her sanity back just in time.
My former former wife has become a unique poet;
most of my work,
such as it is   is done.
Full moon was October second this year,
I ate a mooncake, slept out on the deck,
white light beaming through the black boughs of the pine,
owl hoots and rattling antlers,
Castor and Pollux rising strong
—it's good to know that the Pole Star drifts!
that even our present night sky slips away;
not that I'll see it.
Or maybe I will, much later,
some far time walking the spirit path in the sky,
that long walk of spirits—where you fall right back into the
"narrow painful passageway of the Bardo"

squeeze your little skull
and there you are again
waiting for your ride

. . .

JIM HARRISON: I used to tell students when they were being unpleasant, "The difference between poetry and you is you look in the mirror and say, 'I'm getting old,' right, but Shakespeare looks at the mirror and says, 'Devouring time, blunt thou thy lion's paws.'"

GARY SNYDER: A traveling Zen monk en route from his home monastery back to his home temple, even today, has a traveling bag that he wears around his neck and sewed into it are some ten-thousand-yen notes. Those are to pay for his cremation if he somehow dies on the road.

JIM HARRISON: Wow. That's a real—those are not to be a bother.

GARY SNYDER: Not to be a bother.
    I was hiking in the Sierra high country on scree and talus fields one time, looking, you know, at my feet.

JIM HARRISON: Yeah.

GARY SNYDER: And I noticed then, every rock was different.

JIM HARRISON: Sure.

GARY SNYDER: There were no two little rocks the same, so, you know, there is no—maybe no identity in the whole universe.

JIM HARRISON: That's an intriguing idea.

GARY SNYDER:

They're Listening

As the crickets' soft autumn hum
is to us
so are we to the trees

as are they

to the rocks and the hills.

PART THREE

Outtakes

Further Talks: Gary Snyder and Jim Harrison

Outtakes: Shoemaker/Slovic/Kyger/McClure

Further Talks:
Gary Snyder and Jim Harrison

&

JIM HARRISON: The demographics of my readers—I suppose the same is true for you—it's people in pockets, in rural places.

GARY SNYDER: That doesn't surprise me.

JH: Because if you haven't worked, how would you understand *Riprap?*

GS: Oh well, then you wouldn't understand it if you had! That's a little too esoteric . . .

There's a guy who recently wrote an essay on *Riprap*—I just looked at it, it hasn't been published yet—and I think he kind of went over the top: "Nobody writes about work like Snyder does" . . . I don't think that's quite true . . . if it were true, it would be surprising.

. . .

GS: My poetry is accused of being too simple, but I did have a model, which was Chinese classical poetry, and also Old English.

JH: René Char said, "Lucidity is the wound closest to the sun." I'm not sure what it means, but it's beautiful. Also, "Death thou comest when I had the least of mind"—that's from *Everyman*, twelfth century. What could be simpler than that?

. . .

JH: We make poetry out of our lives. Whereas novels come more out of stories and research, poetry is of the essence of life.

GS: It could be, yeah—and of the language. A compression and stiff focus right into what the language can even be.

JH: Of course it has to be qualified, in your earlier poetry, by the idea that it comes out of the essential near-wildness of work and the rhythm of work.

GS: Yes, but that was just daily labor—in a sense, it just so happened that it was in the backcountry. And the reason it was in the backcountry was that that was where I wanted to be. Period.

. . .

JH: Were you walking when you were seven?

GS: Yeah.

JH: And today, your neurons reconstruct that scene.

GS: Absolutely.

JH: We remember our first paths, Bruce Chatwin said, with our unsureness.

GS: And they could be in the ghetto—this alley, that alley. That garbage can, that mean old lady, or that mean old dog.

JH: Truly.

GS: Turn left at the dog.

JH: If you're talking about "wilderness" and you don't know the content of the twenty-acre wood lot right outside, you know—

GS: Yeah, start there.

JH: There's wildness in certain wood lots that's extraordinary.

. . .

JH: A couple of years ago I began an experiment, and started asking people where they thought they lived historically, botanically, geographically.

GS: That gives you a real interesting start for community education. It gives you a new definition of community, too—like you say, the community is the whole neighborhood in which you clench the nonhuman. And then learning the birds and the flowers is not just high school science or nature study— it's local etiquette. It's rude not to know your neighbors, you know?

JH: In Michigan I knew a marvelous science teacher who knew everything in that region, from raptors to plants—and the kids, once they're told what to pay attention to, just completely eat it up. So I would have county road construction workers stop and talk to me about what birds they'd seen that day, just because of that teacher.

GS: So it involves everybody; it's not discriminatory. I know in our local school, on San Juan Ridge in Nevada County several teachers have been getting guys who work part-time as loggers to come in and talk about what they see in the woods. They see a lot.

. . .

JH: For twenty years in the American Midwest I visited the same forest area because there was a goshawk nest there. They would chase my dogs. Anyway, one day I saw something there that I couldn't quite digest—it was strange, and I finally realized I was looking at a mature signal tree. Of course, we don't have much change in altitude in the Midwest, so the Anishinabes would make signal trees—you take a young sapling and bend it and tie it in a kind of little knot. And that marked your path.

GS: And you looked up to see it.

JH: And I looked up to what had become of a signal tree eighty or ninety years later. It was amazing, in a very unnatural shape, a manmade shape—probably one of the signal trees between two Native American communities, maybe fifteen miles apart.

GS: I never heard of that.

JH: Yeah, it's just in the Midwest because of course, say in California, you can't get lost, because of the changes in altitude.

GS: Not if you pay attention.

. . .

JH: My brother, before he died, went on sabbatical to a very heavily populated area in Crete, and he found there a garden owned by this privately wealthy family, a garden full of plants he had never seen. And it turns out this garden had been in continuous cultivation within this family for eighteen hundred years. They had been maintained in a particular way for over a millennium.

GS: And if they quit maintaining them, they'd be wild again within a few decades.

JH: Maybe that's the virtue of what you're calling "the wild"—to think that this garden is wilder than anything you have in the whole state of Rhode Island, this park in Paris, say.

GS: There's some pretty wild brushlands on the edge of the freeway in New Jersey. Vegetation has the ability to go its own direction anytime.

. . .

GS: When I was teaching poetry, I said to my classes, "If you are into writing poetry because you think it's a career, it's not. This is not the right class for you. You should take the class for fiction or creative nonfiction because you can actually make a living doing that kind of writing if you're really good at it, and persistent; but if you want to study poetry, don't give up your day job."

I said to them, "The best I can provide you with is a hunting license for poetry, but the rest is up to you."

. . .

JH: What Charles Olson said, that a poet should traffic only in his own sign—I asked you about that, and you weren't sure what Olson meant.

GS: Maybe he meant astrologically.

. . .

JH: I was thinking of the idea that your personality becomes less valuable as you age. In fact, it can be a source of irritation when you have to do interviews, because that is the nature of the American literary press.

GS: That's all they've got to talk about. It's easy to talk about.

JH: The age of gossip, in that sense—

GS: Yeah, personal oddities and quirks, and errors you might have made.

JH: I was thinking of what Robert Duncan said about Olson: he said, "Charles wants to go up on the mountain and come back down with twelve new laws once a week." Isn't that marvelous?

GS: Yeah, that is marvelous. I would allow Duncan to say that.

· · ·

GS: So did Duncan ever get free of his personality?

JH: No, but he was very comic about it. He carried it so lightly.

GS: And he made it foolish sometimes.

JH: That's what Denise Levertov couldn't stand about him, his sense of humor. He was so poetic, how comically he could speak about things—he said, "There is a real but everything is mostly exceptions." He was a bit bent on that.

GS: I remember seeing Robert selling one of his books, the latest copy, standing on the sidewalk right out in front of City Lights, selling his own book with a little sign that he made, and whoever I was with said, "Robert Duncan, what are you doing standing out here selling your own books?" "I love to sell my books," he replied.

JH: Yeah right. That would be very Robert. He and my wife liked each other a great deal. John Cage was over when Robert stayed with us at Stony Brook, and to listen to those two banter was extraordinary.

· · ·

JH: I was thinking again about that idea of trying to get rid of a personality that can get in your way, in your public life. Then I thought again of Jack Spicer's deathbed statement: "My vocabulary did this to me."

GS: What did he mean by that?

JH: I think it means the total structure of his life. That was his specific alphabet—the alphabet of his life.

GS: The system, the habitat—

JH: The habitat was his alphabet, but if that included the two bottles of booze a day that killed him, you know—

GS: I have been puzzling over that for many years, what Jack said. Of course, we knew that Jack really knew a lot about language, and knew a lot about what an alphabet might be.

JH: I've thought a lot about the permutations of it, what he said— because certain languages quite efficiently leave out our prized ideas. There's no word for certain of our values—

GS: Ah, but you can say anything in any language if you really want to, if you do it with images.

.   .   .

JH: I was interviewed by a Frenchman, and he asked me—I would never get this question in America—he asked me if I had been influenced by the early poems of Robinson Jeffers. And I said, "Yeah, I read them faithfully in the ninth grade."

GS: I learned a few years ago that a new volume of his selected poems was translated into Polish and went on the market in Poland and proceeded to sell more copies than Robinson Jeffers has sold in the United States in the last twenty years. You know, there is something about Europe.

JH: France has four times fewer people than America, and some of my books have sold ten times as much over there. Who knows why? I took courses in comparative literature, but no one seems to have figured out why one culture adopts the product of another culture.

.   .   .

JH: But also you know a writer is a bit of a shaman with a portfolio. If you can't occupy other people, how can you write? You have to occupy other spirits, other people.

. . .

CREW: But it is interesting why cave painters, for example, didn't portray humanistic scenes.

GS: Not in paintings. But in stories—the stories have plenty of human stuff.

CREW: Maybe animals were less controversial.

CREW: That's what I was trying to get at. Those human beings are just another animal.

GS: And we have a cultural resistance to accepting that story.

CREW: I just think that people are taking inspiration from their needs, and in a Paleolithic environment, it's a very different ecology, and they are surrounded by forces of nature . . .

GS: Maybe Paleolithic people also thought, We people are different from those animals. And, they were totally outnumbered.

. . .

CREW: I'm sure there were narcissistic cave people.

GS: They didn't have mirrors.

. . .

CREW: I just think that there is always an alpha male in every—

GS: There's an alpha female too.

. . .

JH: There was a Zen master—my memory is fading—who said, "Since we're all going to die, don't make a big deal about rehearsing a little bit every morning."

GS: I know that story—the monk who got into his empty coffin every morning and laid in it for a little while. Just practicing, to see what it would feel like. And then he got out and made breakfast.

JH: And also those apocryphal stories of the really old masters who dug their own graves, and then when it was time, jumped in and died. Or like César Vallejo saying, "I'm going to die in Paris on a rainy Thursday," which of course he did.

GS: That's another Zen saying: live as though you have already died.

. . .

WILL HEARST: Did you deal with the S.F. Zen Center at all? Were you involved with Suzuki?

GS: I knew Suzuki Shunryu. When I first got back from Kyoto and lived for a while on Pine Street with my baby son and my Japanese wife, we invited him over for lunch and talked in Japanese. He was charming and wonderful. I knew a lot of the students at the S.F. Zen Center, but between Suzuki and me, we thought, Americans don't have much of a sense of humor, do they? He thought everybody was a little too serious. But he said, "I can't seem to do anything about it."

WH: I'm not sure all that he put into it is blossoming now. It feels a bit down-at-the-heels.

GS: Too serious, and a little too correct.

. . .

GS: The S.F. Zen Center has not really resolved what their relationship to Japan and Japanese Buddhism is; they have not resolved whether or not Buddhist priests should be married or not married. And this is also a problem in Japan. Of course, there's clandestine or unapproved sex in Japan, too, but they know enough not to talk about it. The idea that everything should be out in the open and that we should expose all the difficulties is an American idea—maybe a liberal American idea.

. . .

CREW: How did a good Catholic like Jack Kerouac get interested in Buddhism?

GS: I think it was his confused sexuality.

CREW: I don't follow.

GS: I don't either, but that's what I think it was.

CREW: Gary's articulated this elsewhere—that perhaps certain of the great Buddhist saints kind of played the same role for him as Catholic saints.

JH: Or maybe it was transference.

CREW: Right. But it was also on a much larger timescale.

GS: Oh, Jack loved that huge timescale of Buddhism.

. . .

WH: The picture one gets from Jack Kerouac's books and such from the '50s is that it was a very libertine culture. People felt sexually free. Is that true?

GS: It's historically true in that it was part of the tradition of bohemianism, which of course was imported: Thomas Jefferson loved Paris because it was bohemian and had lots of wine. Charles Sanders Peirce loved Paris, but when he tried to live that bohemian life on the Atlantic seaboard, it wasn't so successful. Things loosened up somewhat in the '50s. It was part of this tiny line of transmission of a certain kind of behavioral freedom, which was experimental in a way—it was related to deliberate utopian experimentalism.

Theoretically, there was gender freedom, but later on many women said, "Well, we all talk about gender freedom in these bohemian circles, but the truth is the men still have the power."

The very first feminist article I read was in a magazine called *Liberation*, which I had a subscription to while living in Kyoto. "We are tired of making coffee," it read; "all this talk about liberation has not really yet applied to women—even in the left, even in the far left, in the anarchist left or in the pacifist left." So that was near the beginning of radical feminism. We were all somewhere in the middle of its development.

WH: It just seems such an important part of the literature: I think of Allen, I think of Jack, parties, girls, dope—

GS: Not really.

WH: That doesn't seem to have been a big part of your scene.

GS: Well, it was red wine. Dope didn't come in till a bit later. But you know, modern American society, as presented in the media and in movies and newspapers and everything, is much wilder than we ever were.

. . .

GS: Captain Cook, sailing around the Pacific in order to be the very first person out of Western culture to contact a lot of different island people, said the one thing that they really got interested in was nails. It was a really good trade item.

And Ishi says that the best thing the white man invented was glue, because it makes it so much easier to finish an arrow.

JH: Maybe our great inventions are the corkscrew and toilet paper, more so than space stations—of real value to man.

. . .

JH: You know, those great floods everywhere in the U.S. around 1900 or so were actually caused by the cutting of eighteen million acres of timber in the north. It lost all its watersheds.

GS: Those big floods down the Mississippi, you mean?

JH: Yeah. They cut all the timber in Northern Michigan, Wisconsin, and Minnesota. So naturally, rather than the slow race to the Mississippi, there were floods. It wasn't an act of God. It was an act of us.

. . .

JH: There are only three days a month that I have to do something, so why not leave me with just three days a month? I mean, who needs all these days?

. . .

GS: Who are my favorite writers? Nobody's asked me that in years. It's not a question I respond to. As a rule.

Outtakes:
Shoemaker/Slovic/Kyger/McClure

❧

I met Gary a long time ago in unusual circumstances. In high school I used to bag groceries at a small grocery store called Scolari's, and on Saturday we had a favorite customer who would come in, and us bag boys would all rush over to be the first one to bag her groceries because we could carry them to her small Airstream trailer about a block away and she would tip us well and tell us outrageous stories. The Airstream trailer kind of looked like a Tom Waits set. There was an open door and a screen door, and behind the screen door you could see a little old man dressed in a wifebeater sitting on the edge of the built-in bed and the place was filled with newspapers, and she was always telling us stories about "my son the poet, my son the poet." And you could never tell with Lois, about her stories, which were true and which weren't. Clearly some of them weren't, but obviously some of them had to be.

In about 1963 I took the obligatory trip to City Lights. At that stage City Lights was much smaller than it is now and all the poetry was downstairs in a little alcove, and I went down to the alcove and there was a copy of *Riprap* by Gary Snyder. So I bought it and I took it back to Santa Maria and I told all my colleagues, "Look, there really is a person named Gary Snyder; she's been telling us the truth—at least about him. And Gary Snyder would come back periodically—having always been a great believer in filial piety, he always was very faithful to his mother and took care of her, coming back periodically from Japan. A few years later I was able with some other people to open a bookstore called the Unicorn in Isla Vista, which is just outside of U.C. Santa Barbara. I was still seeing Lois as often as I could, and a couple of other staff members were also being sure they saw to and took care of her. Eventually I wrote to her son at Daitoku-ji and said, "We're going to open this bookstore, and when you next come to see your mom, would you do the opening poetry reading?" And he wrote back and said he would be delighted to, and around that time Lois got a copy of a handwritten poem of Gary's, and she said, "Oh, I wish I had copies of this to give to my friends." And this was a long time before Xerox, it was the time of carbon paper, and for entirely extraneous reasons I happened to have a Gestetner tabletop offset press in my bedroom and a stencil maker. And so I said, "We'll make copies for you," and we took the poem, "The Bed in the Sky"—it starts off, "Motorcycle strums the empty streets." It's a beautiful poem, and my friend Chuck Miller tried to mimic Gary's calligraphy on the stencil, and we made twenty-six copies and gave them to Lois for her friends.

It's interesting to me that my first act of publishing was pirating Gary. I didn't have his permission, I didn't have a copyright, we didn't even think in those terms—but from that introduction he came and did a wonderful reading at the Unicorn, and I've been Gary's editor and publisher since.

Jack Shoemaker

· · ·

I met Gary for the first time around 1995 or 1996 when I became a professor at the University of Nevada, Reno. Gary came over to do some presentations on campus. One of my strongest memories from that particular experience was having dinner with him at a pub in Sparks, Nevada, and thinking of him as this very thoughtful, deliberate Buddhist, and I know many people who come from sort of a Zen background who are very fastidious eaters, very careful in their personal habits, and at this pub the first thing he did was order a cheeseburger. I love the image of Gary sitting in a pub, a very noisy pub, just having a lively conversation, just a friendly ordinary person eating a cheeseburger, able to produce wonderful literature, extremely thoughtful, and capable of carrying on abstract reflections and conversations but also very down-to-earth.

Scott Slovic

. . .

Someone like Snyder, who was really interested in the intellect, and who prided himself on his curiosity, was fortunate in having as friends Philip Whalen, (who was very erudite and a bit older) and Lew Welch. The three of them prided themselves on their intellectual skills, their literary know-how, and their scholarly approach. They wanted to shine. There was a competitive edge.

Joanne Kyger

. . .

The New American Poetry anthology by Don Allen was a critically important watershed book for a lot of people. It was also very clear to a lot of us that the literary arts, the arts in general, occupied a place of spiritual practice for a whole bunch of people who had been disaffected from normal spiritual activity. Most of us were backslid Christians of one kind or another. My people were all Southern Baptists, and when you had a break with that faith then it was important to have something to fill that spiritual need with, and literature and the arts became that for a lot of people. Gary was an ideal figure in that anthology. Not only had most of us taken transcendental subjects in high school but we also have been born in and grown up around the idea that the unexamined life was not worth living. Gary was clearly a person who lived a carefully, thoroughly examined life.

Jack Shoemaker

. . .

It's common for us to think of artists in general as people who are so embedded in their own aesthetic universes that they don't really know anything beyond their imagination, and I think one of the

particularly inspiring aspects of Gary's writing is the way he actually looks at things outside of himself. He looks at the physical
world. He knew the physical world, I believe, before he really knew
the textural world and knew the importance of language and the
nuances of artistic creation. He grew up wandering around in rural
Washington State and hiking in the North Cascades, and one of the
things I find especially charming about his writing is the fact that
the physical landscape is not just an artistic ornament. The landscape
is present and is important. A reference to a bird or a tree or a rock
or to dust blowing through the air is a powerful experiential refer-
ent. It brings his audience into the scene and enables us to share a
type of experience that is important. With some writers you get the
sense that they're more interested in the playfulness of language, or
in some kind of symbolic dimension of writing. With Gary, that's
often true; I think there's a playfulness, a genuine humor, but in his
Zen-inflected writing in particular there are often profound ideas
about the way our species conceptualizes itself in its relationship to
the world.

Scott Slovic

. . .

Introducing the term "Turtle Island" to the United States and asking,
How about changing your viewpoint a bit and bringing in Coyote?
Well, Coyote, who's Coyote? One of those things we shoot and
run over in our cars? No, Coyote is a mischief-maker who yaps
and bites you in the ass! Gary introduced this to a lot of people. He
helped pass along knowledge of what the logging industry was doing
to America and everywhere else. Asia was beginning to be uncovered; we were all beginning to realize, thanks to Kenneth Rexroth,
that San Francisco is part of the Pacific Rim, that we have more of
a relationship culturally to Asia than we have to New York or to
London. And if you weigh it out piece by piece, that's probably no
exaggeration.

Michael McClure

. . .

One of the things I've always liked about Gary Snyder's writing about the environment is that he doesn't divorce the environment from social and geopolitical concerns. In fact, in some of his more recent writings from the early twenty-first century on the environment, he writes directly about war. There are some essays from *Back on the Fire*, written in 2003 or so, right on the eve of our invasion of Iraq, where he says, Everyone is up in arms about terrorism, particularly the U.S. administration in 2003, and engaged in a war against the perpetrators of the World Trade Center attacks—but no one is paying attention to the fact that we have long been engaged in a much bigger war based on greed and industrial consumption, and that the war against nature is an ongoing and truly devastating phenomenon. So the war between human societies is linked in Snyder's work to our larger war against the planet that is happening in such subtle and ubiquitous ways that we're hardly even aware of it.

Scott Slovic

.   .   .

There was a contingent of people in the U.S., probably fewer in San Francisco than in most of the country, that was dying to have another war, that could hardly wait to get in there and start "knocking the dominos" before somebody else knocked them over. We were aware of this, and we wanted to stop it, and we also wanted to do something about the environment. At the Six Gallery reading, many of the people who were terribly moved by Allen's "Howl" were even more moved by "A Berry Feast" because it spoke out about things that were deeply troubling to many young men and women of our time: overpopulation, cultural blindnesses that made the Paleolithic invisible to us, that made Asia invisible to us, when, in fact, we lived in an Asian city on the Pacific coast where old men sat in Chinatown playing *erhu* on the curb and you could stop and listen to them play their one-string fiddles.

Michael McClure

.   .   .

I don't think Gary would argue long that he was involved in rebellion, per se—not against his family or against his own background. Lots of his people were Wobblies and anarchists and they came from the political left, but the political left was entirely respectable intellectually, it wasn't something that he had to rebel against. Now McClure came out here from Kansas so he had a lot to deal with; he gets to San Francisco and it's very important that he breaks that Kansas mold, but Ginsberg had an edge to it always—even though Allen, when he first came to San Francisco, was still wearing a suit and tie. He may have railed against Brooks Brothers suits but he was wearing one. So I'm not sure rebellion was the order of the day in the counterculture as much as it became the order of the day once there was an active war. Then there was something you had to react to.

Jack Shoemaker

. . .

The reaction to "A Berry Feast" was particularly surprising to me because I wasn't yet hip to how many of the young painters around the Six Gallery were also woods people who did fire-watching and things like that and understood the poem completely. I understood the poem because I had the same hankering to be closer to Asia, and closer to Native America.

At the Six Gallery reading, it was as if the poets were giving the audience what they wanted to hear. In a funny sense, it was almost as if we had been ventriloquized and were saying to the audience what they wished. They wanted to hear my poem about the death of one hundred whales, gray whales chopped up for cat food; they wanted to hear about the mystery, the vision of Point Lobos; they wanted to hear that there was such a thing as Asian thought; they wanted to hear that those native trees were all used up in those houses they were living in. They wanted to hear all of that.

Michael McClure

. . .

I think Gary is a person who has stayed very close to his early convictions. He found a way of living that he's stayed true to. Growing up on a farm has made him clear about where 'things' come from and go to, in terms of their karmic impact. And you know he's always been a teacher—Jack Spicer used to call him the Boy Scout. "You're off to Marin County with the Boy Scout, huh?" In Japan, he very much wanted to live a basic life, close to the roots. Whereas at that point in Japan, people were really trying to get out of a post-World War II economic depression, and were anxious to be part of Westernization. Gary stubbornly wanted to wear, you know, straw sandals and *mompei*.

Joanne Kyger

. . .

From an early age, growing up in the Pacific Northwest, Gary, I think, was interested in who lived in this place before. His early fascination with native people probably had a lot to do with his experience of particular places. And then as I understand it, Gary's interest in East Asia emerged from his encounters with paintings in museums in Seattle, particularly some famous Chinese scrolls showing mountains and rivers, and, as he put it, one particular scroll from China blew his mind because it was supposed to be China, some faraway place, and it looked a lot like the landscapes he knew from the Pacific Northwest. So I think he was interested in the idea that there could be these distant parts of the world that so closely resembled his familiar and much-loved local landscapes.

Geographical isomorphism is a concept advanced by Alexander von Humboldt—the idea that many different parts of the world are all similar in certain ways—and I think Gary Snyder is interested in geographical and linguistic and conceptual isomorphism, similarities in faraway places. You could say that most of his own artistic project has been to take some of the literary ideas from China and Japan and find their equivalent in the North American vernacular. So when he went to college at Reed, he studied anthropology and began to focus on Native American ideas in a more formal way, which he gradually absorbed into his own artistry and scholarship, conscious of the fact that these intellectual traditions belong to other cultures, but over time absorbing them into his own imagination, into his own poetic voice. In a lot of his work you see an idiosyncratic blend of the indigenous North American point of view and the adopted East Asian vocabulary and perspective curiously mixed together and made into something that he himself possesses.

One of the things I asked him on the occasion when I first met him in the mid-'90s was, "What do you say to people who accuse you of cultural appropriation, who say you're taking all these ideas about Coyote and Raven from people who really come from cultures that have produced a sort of intrinsic meaning for these concepts?" or, "What do you say to people who accuse you of appropriating East Asian Buddhist ideas and kind of playing with them and distorting them in your own West Coast perspective?" I asked him all this. And in a sort of joking way, but in a way that also suggested that he had been accosted with this question in the past, he just smiled and said, "Stop speaking English." If you come from a culture that doesn't normally use English, like from Japan or from a traditional Native American tribe where you once used Paiute or Shoshone or some other language, stop speaking English. It's what the human imagination does. We absorb, we inherit, we put things together; and so by reaching into these other cultures and appreciating them and then distorting and tweaking and fitting them together, and also fitting them with his own direct experience, he is simply exhibiting what the human mind does. All of us do that in one way or another—whenever we have an encounter beyond our sphere of experience, we absorb that encounter and make something of it. The fact that he has done so publicly through his writing may make him a bit of a lightning rod for accusations of cultural appropriation, but he's simply doing what any of us would do, and if anyone were to accuse him of appropriating Japanese culture in some way, that doesn't seem quite correct. Japanese society itself is wonderfully famous for taking ideas from far-flung sources, from India, from China, from the United States, and in a syncretic way, transforming these phenomena and possessing them. So I like that flippant and funny and entirely appropriate response. Stop speaking English.

Scott Slovic

. . .

Gary's sensory perceptions, his outspokenness regarding the environment, I believe have a great deal to do with his mastery of Asian languages: where a number is not in existence, where time is a different frame. Put one way, it's the ability to conceptualize in a language in which things are allowed their immediate appearance as real objects—without the surrounding of social padding that goes with Western languages. And I think that's part of Gary's unique view of nature.

Michael McClure

. . .

The last three lines of Gary's poem "For the Children" are "*stay together / learn the flowers / go light.*"

"Stay together": pay attention to the importance of community. Work with each other. Even if you have opposing perspectives, even if you come from different cultural traditions, find a way to work together to stay together.

"Learn the flowers": notice your surroundings and learn about them. To me, "learn" implies actively studying something—not just learning what it looks like on a superficial level, but actually engaging in an energetic and deliberate effort of study. This, too, is something that I think is very important about Gary's work: he's not operating solely on an aesthetic level he's made an active effort to study the cultural traditions, the languages, and the natural history that he absorbs into his poetry.

And finally, "Go light": pay attention to your actual lifestyle, to the practical aspects of your life. Try to have a light impact on the planet and on the cultural communities that you are intersecting with. "Go light" means "live carefully." So: stay together, learn the flowers, go light. I think many of us who work in the field of literature and environment carry these three lines around with us everywhere we go, with thanks to Gary Snyder.

Scott Slovic

PART FOUR
Poems

꧁

Hay for the Horses

He had driven half the night
From far down San Joaquin
Through Mariposa, up the
Dangerous mountain roads,
And pulled in at eight a.m.
With his big truckload of hay
      behind the barn.
With winch and ropes and hooks
We stacked the bales up clean
To splintery redwood rafters
High in the dark, flecks of alfalfa
Whirling through shingle-cracks of light,
Itch of haydust in the
      sweaty shirt and shoes.
At lunchtime under Black oak
Out in the hot corral,
—The old mare nosing lunchpails,
Grasshoppers crackling in the weeds—
"I'm sixty-eight," he said,
"I first bucked hay when I was seventeen.
I thought, that day I started,
I sure would hate to do this all my life.
And dammit, that's just what
I've gone and done."

Piute Creek

One granite ridge
A tree, would be enough
Or even a rock, a small creek,
A bark shred in a pool.
Hill beyond hill, folded and twisted
Tough trees crammed
In thin stone fractures
A huge moon on it all, is too much.
The mind wanders. A million
Summers, night air still and the rocks
Warm.   Sky over endless mountains.
All the junk that goes with being human
Drops away, hard rock wavers
Even the heavy present seems to fail
This bubble of a heart.
Words and books
Like a small creek off a high ledge
Gone in the dry air.

A clear, attentive mind
Has no meaning but that
Which sees is truly seen.
No one loves rock, yet we are here.
Night chills. A flick
In the moonlight
Slips into Juniper shadow:
Back there unseen
Cold proud eyes
Of Cougar or Coyote
Watch me rise and go.

Water

Pressure of sun on the rockslide
Whirled me in a dizzy hop-and-step descent,
Pool of pebbles buzzed in a Juniper shadow,
Tiny tongue of a this-year rattlesnake flicked,
I leaped, laughing for little boulder-color coil—
Pounded by heat raced down the slabs to the creek
Deep tumbling under arching walls and stuck
Whole head and shoulders in the water:
Stretched full on cobble—ears roaring
Eyes open aching from the cold and faced a trout.

from Myths and Texts

14

The groves are down
          cut down
Groves of Ahab, of Cybele
Pine trees, knobbed twigs
    thick cone and seed
    Cybele's tree this, sacred in groves
Pine of Seami, cedar of Haida
Cut down by the prophets of Israel
    the fairies of Athens
    the thugs of Rome
          both ancient and modern;
Cut down to make room for the suburbs
Bulldozed by Luther and Weyerhaeuser
Crosscut and chainsaw
    squareheads and finns
    high-lead and cat-skidding
Trees down
Creeks choked, trout killed, roads.

Sawmill temples of Jehovah.
Squat black burners 100 feet high
Sending the smoke of our burnt
Live sap and leaf
To his eager nose.

Song of the Taste

Eating the living germs of grasses
Eating the ova of large birds

    the fleshy sweetness packed
    around the sperm of swaying trees

The muscles of the flanks and thighs of
        soft-voiced cows
    the bounce in the lamb's leap
    the swish in the ox's tail

Eating roots grown swoll
      inside the soil

Drawing on life of living
    clustered points of light spun
        out of space
hidden in the grape.

    Eating each other's seed
        eating
  ah, each other.

    Kissing the lover in the mouth of bread:
      lip to lip.

They're Listening

As the crickets' soft autumn hum
is to us
so are we to the trees

as are they

to the rocks and the hills.

Virgin

A virgin forest
      is ancient; many-
      breasted, stable
at climax.

As for Poets

As for poets
The Earth Poets
Who write small poems,
Need no help from no man.

❧

The Air Poets
Play out the swiftest gales
And sometimes loll in their eddies.
Poem after poem,
Curling back on the same thrust.

❧

At fifty below
Fuel oil won't flow
And propane stays in the tank.
Fire Poets
Burn at absolute zero
Fossil love pumped back up.

❧

The first
Water Poet
Stayed down six years.
He was covered with seaweed.
The life in his poem
Left millions of tiny
Different tracks
Criss-crossing through the mud.

With the Sun and Moon
In his belly,
The Space Poet
Sleeps.
No end to the sky—
But his poems,
Like wild geese,
Fly off the edge.

A Mind Poet
Stays in the house.
The house is empty
And it has no walls.
The poem
Is seen from all sides,
Everywhere,
At once.

Ripples on the Surface

"Ripples on the surface of the water—
were silver salmon passing under—different
from the ripples caused by breezes"

A scudding plume on the wave—
a humpback whale is
breaking out in air up
gulping herring
          —Nature not a book, but a *performance*, a
high old culture

Ever-fresh events
scraped out, rubbed out, and used, used, again—
the braided channels of the rivers
hidden under fields of grass—

The vast wild
          the house, alone.
The little house in the wild,
          the wild in the house.
Both forgotten.

                    No nature

          Both together, one big empty house.

Right in the Trail

Here it is, near the house,
A **big** pile, fat scats,
Studded with those deep red
Smooth-skinned manzanita berries,
Such a pile! Such droppings,
Awesome. And I saw how
The young girl in the story,
Had good cause to comment
On the bearscats she found while
Picking blueberries with her friends.
She laughed at them
Or maybe **with** them, jumped over them
(Bad luck!), and is reported
To have said "wide anus!"
To amuse or annoy the Big Brown Ones
Who are listening, of course.

They say the ladies
Have always gone berrying
And they all join together
To go out for the herring spawn,
Or to clean green salmon.
And that big set of lessons
On what bears really want,
Was brought back by the girl
Who made those comments:
She was taken on a year-long excursion
Deep in the mountains,
Through the tangled deadfalls,

Down into the den.
She had some pretty children by a
Young and handsome Bear.

  Now I'm on the dirt
Looking at these scats
And I want to cry not knowing why
At the honor and the humor
Of coming on this sign
That is not found in books
Or transmitted in letters,
And is for women just as much as men,
A shining message for all species,
A glimpse at the Trace
Of the Great One's passing,
With a peek into her whole wild system—
And what was going on last week,
(Mostly still manzanita)—

  Dear Bear: do stay around. Be good.
And though I know
It won't help to say this,

Chew your food.

For Lew Welch in a Snowfall

Snowfall in March:
I sit in the white glow reading a thesis
About you. Your poems, your life.

The author's my student,
He even quotes me.

Forty years since we joked in a kitchen in Portland
Twenty since you disappeared.

All those years and their moments—
Crackling bacon, slamming car doors,
Poems tried out on friends,
Will be one more archive,
One more shaky text.

But life continues in the kitchen
Where we still laugh and cook,
Watching snow.

A Berry Feast

I

Fur the color of mud, the smooth loper
Crapulous old man, a drifter,
Praises! of Coyote the Nasty, the fat
Puppy that abused himself, the ugly gambler,
Bringer of goodies.

   In bearshit find it in August,
   Neat pile on the fragrant trail, in late
   August, perhaps by a Larch tree
   Bear has been eating the berries.
       high meadow, late summer, snow gone
   Blackbear
       eating berries, married
   To a woman whose breasts bleed
   From nursing the half-human cubs.

    Somewhere of course there are people
    collecting and junking, gibbering all day,

"Where I shoot my arrows
"There is the sunflower's shade
      —song of the rattlesnake
      coiled in the boulder's groin
"K'ak, k'ak, k'ak!
      sang Coyote. Mating with
      humankind—
      The Chainsaw falls for boards of pine,
      Suburban bedrooms, block on block

Will waver with this grain and knot,
The maddening shapes will start and fade
Each morning when commuters wake—
Joined boards hung on frames,
                    a box to catch the biped in.

            and the shadow swings around the tree
Shifting on the berrybush
            from leaf to leaf across each day
The shadow swings around the tree.

2

Three, down, through windows
Dawn leaping cats, all barred brown, grey
Whiskers aflame
            bits of mouse on the tongue

Washing the coffeepot in the river
            the baby yelling for breakfast,
Her breasts, black-nippled, blue-veined, heavy,
Hung through the loose shirt
            squeezed, with the free hand
                    white jet in three cups.
Cars at dawn
            derry derry down

Creeks wash clean where trout hide
We chew the black plug
Sleep on needles through long afternoons
            "you shall be owl

"you shall be sparrow
"you will grow thick and green, people
"will eat you, you berries!
Coyote: shot from the car, two ears,
A tail, bring bounty.
    Clanks of tread
        oxen of Shang
        moving the measured road

Bronze bells at the throat
Bronze balls on the horns, the bright Oxen
Chanting through sunlight and dust
      wheeling logs down hills
        into heaps,
            the yellow
     Fat-snout Caterpillar, tread toppling forward
     Leaf on leaf, roots in gold volcanic dirt.

When
Snow melts back
      from the trees
Bare branches   knobbed pine twigs
     hot sun on wet flowers
Green shoots of huckleberry
Breaking through snow.

3

Belly stretched taut in a bulge
Breasts swelling as you guzzle beer, who wants
      Nirvana?

Here is water, wine, beer
Enough books for a week
A mess of afterbirth,
A smell of hot earth, a warm mist
Steams from the crotch

"You can't be killers all your life
"The people are coming—
          —and when Magpie
Revived him, limp rag of fur in the river
Drowned and drifting, fish-food in the shallows,
"Fuck you!" sang Coyote
                    and ran.

Delicate blue-black, sweeter from meadows
Small and tart in the valleys, with light blue dust
Huckleberries scatter through pine woods
Crowd along gullies, climb dusty cliffs,
Spread through the air by birds;
Find them in droppings of bear.

"Stopped in the night
"Ate hot pancakes in a bright room
"Drank coffee, read the paper
"In a strange town, drove on,
          singing, as the drunkard swerved the car
"Wake from your dreams, bright ladies!
"Tighten your legs, squeeze demons from
          the crotch with rigid thighs
"Young red-eyed men will come
"With limp erections, snuffling cries
"To dry your stiffening bodies in the sun!

Woke at the beach. Grey dawn,
Drenched with rain. One naked man
Frying his horsemeat on a stone.

4

Coyote yaps, a knife!
Sunrise on yellow rocks.
People gone, death no disaster,
Clear sun in the scrubbed sky
              empty and bright
Lizards scurry from darkness
We lizards sun on yellow rocks.
    See, from the foothills
    Shred of river glinting, trailing
    To flatlands, the city:
              glare of haze in the valley horizon
    Sun caught on glass gleams and goes.
    From cool springs under cedar
    On his haunches, white grin,
              long tongue panting, he watches:

Dead city in dry summer,
Where berries grow.

Afterword

❦

Grace
From *The Practice of the Wild*

There is a verse chanted by Zen Buddhists called the "Four Great Vows." The first line goes: "Sentient beings are numberless, I vow to save them." *Shujōmuhen seigando.* It's a bit daunting to announce this intention—aloud—to the universe daily. This vow stalked me for several years and finally pounced: I realized that I had vowed to let the sentient beings save *me*. In a similar way, the precept against taking life, against causing harm, doesn't stop in the negative. It is urging us to *give* life, to *undo* harm.

Those who attain some ultimate understanding of these things are called "Buddhas," which means "awakened ones." The word is connected to the English verb "to bud." I once wrote a little parable:

Who the Buddhas Are
All the beings of the universe are already realized. That is, with the exception of one or two beings. In those rare cases the cities, villages, meadows, and forests, with all their birds, flowers, animals, rivers, trees, and humans, that surround such a person, all collaborate to educate, serve, challenge, and instruct such a one, until that person also becomes a New Beginner Enlightened Being. Recently realized beings are enthusiastic to teach and train and start schools and practices. Being able to do this develops their confidence and insight up to the point that they are fully ready to join the seamless world of interdependent

play. Such new enlightened beginners are called "Buddhas" and they like to say things like "I am enlightened together with the whole universe" and so forth.

Boat in a Storm, 1987

Good luck! One might say. The test of the pudding is in the *eating*. It narrows down to a look at the conduct that is entwined with food. At mealtime (seated on the floor in lines) the Zen monks chant:

> Porridge is effective in ten ways
> To aid the student of Zen
> No limit to the good result
> Consummating eternal happiness

and

> Oh, all you demons and spirits
> We now offer this food to you
> May all of you everywhere
> Share it with us together

and

> We wash our bowls in this water
> It has the flavor of ambrosial dew
> We offer it to all demons and spirits
> May all be filled and satisfied
> *Om makula sai svaha*

And several other verses. These superstitious-sounding old ritual formulas are never mentioned in lectures, but they are at the heart of the teaching. Their import is older than Buddhism or any of the world religions. They are part of the first and last practice of the wild: *Grace.*

Everyone who ever lived took the lives of other animals, pulled plants, plucked fruit, and ate. Primary people have had their own ways of trying to understand the precept of nonharming. They knew that taking life required gratitude and care. There is no death that is not somebody's food, no life that is not somebody's death. Some would take this as a sign that the universe is fundamentally flawed. This leads to a disgust with self, with humanity, and with nature. Otherworldly philosophies end up doing more damage to the planet (and human psyches) than the pain and suffering that is in the existential conditions they seek to transcend.

The archaic religion is to kill god and eat him. Or her. The shimmering food-chain, the food-web, is the scary, beautiful condition of the biosphere. Subsistence people live without excuses. The blood is on your own hands as you divide the liver from the gallbladder. You have watched the color fade on the glimmer of the trout. A subsistence economy is a sacramental economy because it has faced up to one of the critical problems of life and death: the taking of life for food. Contemporary people do not need to hunt, many cannot even afford meat, and in the developed world the variety of foods available to us makes the avoidance of meat an easy choice. Forests in the tropics are cut to make pasture to raise beef for the American market. Our distance from the source of our food enables us to be superficially more comfortable, and distinctly more ignorant.

Eating is a sacrament. The grace we say clears our hearts and guides the children and welcomes the guest, all at the same time. We look at eggs, apples, and stew. They are evidence of plenitude, excess, a great reproductive exuberance. Millions of grains of grass-seed that will become rice or flour, millions of codfish fry that will never, and *must* never, grow to maturity. Innumerable little seeds are sacrifices to the food-chain. A parsnip in the ground is a marvel of living chemistry, making sugars and flavors from earth, air, water. And if we do eat meat it is the life, the bounce, the swish, of a great alert being with keen ears and lovely eyes, with foursquare feet and a huge beating heart that we eat, let us not deceive ourselves.

We too will be offerings—we are all edible. And if we are not devoured quickly, we are big enough (like the old downed trees) to provide a long slow meal to the smaller critters. Whale carcasses that sink several miles deep in the ocean feed organisms in the dark for fifteen years. (It seems to take about two thousand to exhaust the nutrients in a high civilization.)

At our house we say a Buddhist grace—

> We venerate the Three Treasures [teachers, the wild, and friends]
> And are thankful for this meal
> The work of many people
> And the sharing of other forms of life.

Anyone can use a grace from their own tradition (and really give it meaning)—or make up their own. Saying some sort of grace is never inappropriate, and speeches and announcements can be tacked onto it. It is a plain, ordinary, old-fashioned little thing to do that connects us with all our ancestors.

> A monk asked Dong-shan: "Is there a practice for people to follow?" Dong-shan answered: "When you become a real person, there is such a practice."

> *Sarvamangalam, Good Luck to All.*

Biographies and Reading Lists

| | |

GARY SNYDER was born in San Francisco and grew up in rural Washington, where he acquired wilderness training at an early age and developed keen interests in the native cultures of the Pacific Northwest. He attended Reed College, where he met poets Philip Whalen and Lew Welch while studying literature and Pacific Northwest folklore, and worked intermittently as all fire lookout and all forestry hand.

After briefly pursuing graduate studies in Linguistics at Indiana University, Snyder returned to San Francisco devoted himself to poetry and Buddhist studies. He entered Graduate School at U.C. Berkeley in the Department of East Asian Languages where he studied Chinese poetry with Chen Shih-hsiang and did his Han-shan translations. Kenneth Rexroth soon introduced Allen Ginsberg to Gary, initiating a long friendship; both participated in the famous Six Gallery reading, where Ginsberg first read "Howl" and Snyder "A Berry Feast," on October 7, 1955. After living in Marin County in preparation for his travels, Snyder left for Japan later that year, where he lived for the majority of the next decade as a *koji* (lay adept) with Oda Sesso Roshi at Daitoku-ji Monastery, and as apprentice to the translator Ruth Fuller Sasaki. *Riprap*, Snyder's first book of poems, was published in 1959. He and poet Joanne Kyger were married in 1960 and, along with Ginsberg and Peter Orlovsky, traveled widely in India; the experience resulted in Snyder's *Passage Through India*. In 1966 Snyder, Ginsberg, and Dick Baker purchased one hundred acres on the South Yuba River in the Northern Sierra foothills, on which the Snyder home was built by hand and christened Kitkitdizze in 1970.

Turtle Island was published in 1974; it won the Pulitzer Prize for Poetry in 1975. The title reintroduced to modern America an evocative indigenous name for the North American continent, and in this and other ways Snyder participated in and inspired various environmental movements of the time, including Earth Day, Deep Ecology, the Native American movement, and the reinhabitation/"back to the land" diaspora of the American west. Throughout the 1980s and 1990s, Snyder wrote essays and lectured widely, both as professor at U.C. Davis and at conferences across the world, developing these many strains of interest into the concept of bioregionalism. Snyder is a community advocate/activist in the Yuba River watershed, where he still lives at Kitkitdizze.

POETRY
Riprap and Cold Mountain Poems
Myths and Texts
The Back Country
Regarding Wave
Turtle Island
Axe Handles
Left Out in the Rain
No Nature
Mountains and Rivers Without End
Danger on Peaks

PROSE
Earth House Hold
He Who Hunted Birds in His Father's Village
The Real Work
Passage Through India
The Practice of the Wild
A Place in Space
The High Sierra of California (with Tom Killion)
Back on the Fire
Tamalpais Walking (with Tom Killion)

POETRY AND PROSE SELECTIONS
The Gary Snyder Reader
Look Out: A Selection of Writings
The Selected Letters of Allen Ginsberg and Gary Snyder (Bill Morgan, ed.)

JIM HARRISON was born in Grayling, Michigan and educated at Michigan State University, where he received degrees in comparative literature. A brief spell as assistant professor at SUNY Stony Brook was followed, in 1966, by his transition to full-time writer. He was fascinated by the human drama of place, particularly his own native American Midwest, and his work evokes and argues for a naturalism of human affairs. He has published widely for four decades in as many genres. Beginning with *Plain Song* (1965), he has published more than seventeen books of poetry, most recently *In Search of Small Gods* (Copper Canyon, 2009). Harrison's novellas were first published in *Legends of the Fall* (1979), the title novella of which was adapted to film in 1994. Perhaps the most regarded among his many novels, *Dalva*, both a rural Nebraskan family saga and a threnody for the Plains Indian way of life, was published in 1988. His essays and other nonfiction writings have been collected in 1991's *Just Before Dark*. A children's book, *The Boy Who Ran to the Woods*, was published in 2000 with illustrations by Tom Pohrt.

His work has appeared in *The New Yorker, Esquire, Rolling Stone, Playboy*, and *Sports Illustrated*, among many other publications. He is the recipient of three National Academy of Arts grants and a Guggenheim Fellowship; in 2007, he was elected to the Academy of American Arts and Letters. He lives in Arizona and Montana.

FICTION
Wolf: A False Memoir
A Good Day to Die
Farmer
Warlock
Sundog: The Story of an American Foreman, Robert Corvus Strang
Dalva
The Road Home
True North
Returning to Earth
The English Major

NOVELLA TRILOGIES
Legends of the Fall
The Woman Lit by Fireflies
Julip
The Beast God Forgot to Invent
The Summer He Didn't Die
The Farmer's Daughter

CHILDREN'S LITERATURE
The Boy Who Ran to the Woods

POETRY
Plain Song
Locations
Outlyer and Ghazals
Letters to Yesenin
Returning to Earth
Selected and New Poems, 1961–1981
The Theory & Practice of Rivers and New Poems
After Ikkyu and Other Poems
The Shape of the Journey: New and Collected Poems
Braided Creek: A Conversation in Poetry (with Ted Kooser)
Saving Daylight
In Search of Small Gods

NONFICTION
Just Before Dark: Collected Nonfiction
The Raw and the Cooked: Adventures of a Roving Gourmand
Off to the Side: A Memoir

THE PRACTICE OF THE WILD
A Conversation with Gary Snyder and Jim Harrison
San Simeon Films

Directed by
JOHN J. HEALEY

Produced by
WILL HEARST
JIM HARRISON

Associate Producers
CYNTHIA LUND
JOHN GOECKE

Director of Photography
ALISON KELLY

Editor
ROBIN LEE

Sound Recordist
CLAUDIA KATAYANAGI

First Assistant Camera
AARON SCHUH

Additional Camera Operators
CEDRIC MARTIN
DAVID SHEETZ
AARON SCHUH

Gaffer
DAVID SHEETZ

Digital Imaging Technician
JOSH TAUBENSEE

Sound Assistant
JOAN HALAPUA WOOD

Assistant Editor
STEVEN FARR

Archivist
LISA NEINCHEL

Titles
TONY HUDSON

Supervising Sound Editor
TERESA ECKTON

Re-recording Mixer
CHRISTOPHER BARNETT

Sound Assistant
ANGIE YESSON

Legal Services
GLENN NASH
EZRA J. DONER

Chief Wrangler
BILL FLEMION

Catering
ANTHONY SCORSONE, HEAD CHEF
MITCH SCORSONE
JASON SUMMERHAYS
SCOTT WATTERS

The producers wish to thank the following for their contribution:

SCOTT SLOVIC
Author, and Head of Literature and Environment,
University of Nevada, Reno

JACK SHOEMAKER
Editorial Director, Counterpoint

MICHAEL MCCLURE
Poet and Musician

JOANNE KYGER
Poet and Author

*Special thanks to Sunical Land and Livestock
for permission to shoot on Rancho Piedra Blancas.*

Special Mention
GEN SNYDER
STEVE HEARST
CLIFF GARRISON
COURTNEY WARNER